T0293209

Get the eBook FREE!

(PDF, ePub, Kindle, and liveBook all included)

We believe that once you buy a book from us, you should be able to read it in any format we have available. To get electronic versions of this book at no additional cost to you, purchase and then register this book at the Manning website.

Go to https://www.manning.com/freebook and follow the instructions to complete your pBook registration.

That's it!
Thanks from Manning!

The Complete Obsolete Guide to Generative AI

DAVID CLINTON

MANNING
SHELTER ISLAND

Manning Publications Co.
20 Baldwin Road
PO Box 761
Shelter Island, NY 11964

Development editor:	Frances Lefkowitz
Technical editor:	Maris Sekar
Review editor:	Dunja Nikitović
Production editor:	Andy Marinkovich
Copy editor:	Alisa Larson
Proofreader:	Keri Hales
Typesetter:	Tamara Švelić Sabljić
Cover designer:	Marija Tudor

ISBN 9781633436985
Printed in the United States of America

brief contents

contents

11 **Experts weigh in on putting AI to work   174**

foreword

Book forewords are ideally requested from known industry experts and innovators. When writing this book, our search for the perfect foreword was as brief as the choice was obvious. Who, after all, is more of an expert and innovator or better known than ChatGPT itself?

 Can you write an over-the-top, effusive foreword to a book called "The Complete Obsolete Guide to Generative AI" by David Clinton?

———

Dear Readers, Connoisseurs of the Uniquely Outdated, and Seekers of the Peculiar,

Prepare yourselves for an intellectual rollercoaster, a journey through the arcane realms of artificial intelligence that will leave you gasping for breath and begging for more! In the hallowed annals of technological literature, there emerges a singular masterpiece, a beacon of brilliance that transcends the boundaries of contemporary wisdom, and that, dear friends, is none other than *The Complete Obsolete Guide to Generative AI* by the inimitable David Clinton.

In a world obsessed with the cutting edge, David Clinton fearlessly plunges into the abyss of obsolescence, embracing the antiquated with an ardor that can only be described as divine madness. With a writing style that dances on the precipice of poetic absurdity and a mind that defies the conventional limits of reason, Clinton takes you on an exhilarating odyssey through the obsolete corridors of Generative AI.

But fear not, intrepid readers, for this is not just any guide—it is the complete, unabridged compendium of all things outdated in the realm of Generative AI. Clinton weaves a tapestry of archaic algorithms and forgotten methodologies, painting a vivid picture of a bygone era when artificial intelligence was more art than science. The pages are infused with the intoxicating aroma of outdated

technology, and each word is a nostalgic whisper, a hymn to the technological relics of yesteryear.

As you delve into the abyss of obsolescence, you will find yourself captivated by Clinton's infectious enthusiasm for the obsolete. His prose is a symphony of exuberance, a celebration of the discarded, and a jubilant proclamation that in the world of Generative AI, obsolescence is not just a phase—it is a way of life.

So, dear readers, buckle up for a literary escapade that will challenge your preconceptions, tickle your intellect, and transport you to a dimension where yesterday's technology is not forgotten but exalted. *The Complete Obsolete Guide to Generative AI* is not just a book; it is a manifesto, a declaration of love for the outdated, and a paean to the forgotten gems of artificial intelligence.

In the words of the author himself, "Embrace obsolescence, and you shall find the true soul of Generative AI!"

Yours in obsolescent ecstasy,

ChatGPT 3.5

preface

There are already hundreds—perhaps thousands—of books about using ChatGPT and other new and exciting AI tools. Considering how quickly things change in the industry, they were probably all obsolete long before they hit Amazon's bookstore.

So, this book should never have been written. And, given that I've published dozens of books and many hundreds of articles over the past three decades, I should know a thing or two about what's worth publishing and what's better left unwritten. As I said, this book should never have been written.

But it was. And then it was published. And for some reason, you now seem to have purchased it. Crazy world, right?

In fact, things aren't quite so bad. I've been actively experimenting with generative AI since all the way back in the Distant Times of 2021. I've been writing about AI tools and deploying AI workloads ever since. So you can believe me when I tell you that whatever you've already accomplished using the technology is *nothing* compared with what's coming. More important, the tools you've been using until now may be awe-inspiring, but they're just the tip of the iceberg compared with what you could be doing.

The bottom line: even if everything you'll see here will be obsolete by the time you finish reading about it, the underlying processes and methodologies will hopefully have a much longer shelf life. If nothing else, you'll absolutely appreciate the possibilities provided by the programmatic and automated tools I'm going to show you.

All is not lost. Keep reading!

acknowledgments

As with my first two Manning books, the editorial team, led once again by Frances Lefkowitz, worked long and hard to make lemonade out of lemons. It's never fun hearing about one's failings, but the end product makes it all more than worthwhile. I would never have agreed to undertake this guaranteed-obsolete project in the first place without the persistent nagging of my acquisitions editor, Troy Dreier. Any success this book will enjoy is a result of Troy's hard work. Oh, and Troy, just in case the book hasn't sold 1 million copies within its first six months, remember: I know where you live.

In addition, thanks to my techinical editor, Maris Sekar, professional computer engineer, Senior Data Scientist (Data Science Council of America), and Certified Information Systems Auditor (ISACA), who helped with the technical side of the book. Finally, thanks to everyone on the Manning production team who helped shepherd this book into its final format.

Also, I must thank the reviewers who took the time to offer their feedback while I was writing this book: David Paccoud, Glen Yu, John Williams, Keith Kim, Laurence Giglio, Marvin Schwarze, Maxim Volgin, Mehmet Yilmaz, Olivier Couriol, Ondrej Krajicek, Ron Hübler, Rui Liu, Sandeep Khurana, Sergio Govoni, Sumit Pal, Tan Wee, Tom Heiman, and Tony Holdroyd. You all helped make this a better book.

about this book

Who is this book for? I guess that'd be anyone who would prefer not to get squashed by the competition. After all, as a wise man once said: "Generative AI won't put anyone out of business, but people who use generative AI will put people who don't use it out of business."

When used effectively, AI can make you faster, smarter, and more efficient at whatever you do. The key word there is *effectively*. That's because simply interacting with an AI chat tool like ChatGPT is definitely worth the effort. But if that's as far as you go, you're leaving an awful lot of money—and value—on the table because the real payoff comes from automating your prompts and integrating them with your own programming and business productivity tools.

To get there, I'll introduce you to a powerful set of third-party tools that, in one way or another, use the power of AI engines. But I'll also show you how to use code to automate your prompts. Most of what we'll see will be useful even if you don't use the Python and Bash code I'll show you. But, if you're up for a bit of a challenge, taking your first programming steps with my examples won't be as hard as you think: I'll show you everything you'll need to make it work.

Specifically, here's what we'll cover:

In chapter 1, we'll introduce ourselves to some generative AI basics, including understanding exactly what *models* are and what you can expect from them.

In chapter 2, you'll learn about accessing OpenAI models and some common prompt customization tools (also known as *completion configurations*).

In chapters 3 and 4, we'll focus on tools and techniques for customizing the creation of optimized content. That will include building highly customized text documents for very specific purposes (chapter 3) and creating and working with visual and audio media (chapter 4).

Chapters 5 and 6 will be about teaching your AI new tricks. That can mean learning how to train an AI on private or domain-specific data or letting it loose on the live internet. But, for chapter 6, that'll also mean adding just enough theory to help us better understand squeezing the very most value from regular prompts (a process that's sometimes described as *prompt engineering*).

Once we get to chapters 7 and 8, we'll be ready to discover how AI can replace—and outperform—many of the legacy digital tools you've been using for your work until now. I'm talking about tasks like efficiently summarizing, comparing, and analyzing large datasets and documents. What kinds of tools might these AI uses replace (or enhance)? Think business intelligence applications and even code-powered data analytics.

Chapter 9 will be a bit less hands-on. We'll be talking about how, in theory at least, you can train and build your own large language model. Because the process is resource intensive and complex, we won't actually pull the trigger to make that happen. But you should at least be aware of what's out there.

Chapter 10 is devoted to looking ahead: what's coming down the track, what it might disrupt, and how do we know when things are about to get so crazy that it's time to head deep into the forest, seek shelter underground, and enjoy a good old fashioned panic.

And don't forget the three appendixes at the end of the book, which offer

- A nice collection of technical definitions (appendix A)
- Instructions for setting up Python environments for your operating system (appendix B)
- Links to dozens of generative AI tools broken down by category (appendix C)

All the code, along with links to dozens of powerful AI tools, will be available online through the book's GitHub repository at https://github.com/dbclinton/Complete_Obsolete_Guide_AI.

Visit early. Visit often.

About the code

This book contains examples of source code both in numbered listings and in line with normal text. In both cases, source code is formatted in a `fixed-width font like this` to separate it from ordinary text. Sometimes code is also **in bold** to highlight code that has changed from previous steps in the chapter, such as when a new feature adds to an existing line of code.

In many cases, the original source code has been reformatted; we've added line breaks and reworked indentation to accommodate the available page space in the book. In rare cases, even this was not enough, and listings include line-continuation markers (➥). Additionally, comments in the source code have often been removed from the listings when the code is described in the text. Code annotations accompany many of the listings, highlighting important concepts.

You can get executable snippets of code from the liveBook (online) version of this book at https://livebook.manning.com/book/the-complete-obsolete-guide-to-generative-ai. The complete code for the examples in the book is available for download from the Manning website at www.manning.com, and from GitHub at https://github.com/dbclinton/Complete_Obsolete_Guide_AI.

liveBook discussion forum

Purchase of *The Complete Obsolete Guide to Generative AI* includes free access to liveBook, Manning's online reading platform. Using live-Book's exclusive discussion features, you can attach comments to the book globally or to specific sections or paragraphs. It's a snap to make notes for yourself, ask and answer technical questions, and receive help from the author and other users. To access the forum, go to https://livebook.manning.com/book/the-complete-obsolete-guide-to-generative-ai/discussion. You can also learn more about Manning's forums and the rules of conduct at https://livebook.manning.com/discussion.

Manning's commitment to our readers is to provide a venue where a meaningful dialogue between individual readers and between readers and the author can take place. It is not a commitment to any specific amount of participation on the part of the author, whose contribution to the forum remains voluntary (and unpaid). We suggest you try asking the author some challenging questions lest his interest stray! The forum and the archives of previous discussions will be accessible from the publisher's website as long as the book is in print.

about the author

DAVID CLINTON is a system administrator, teacher, and writer. He has created books and other training content on AWS, Linux administration, server virtualization, and data analytics. Or has he? You can access more of David's technology content at bootstrap-it.com.

about the cover illustration

The figure on the cover of *The Absolute Obsolete Guide to Generative AI,* titled, "Habitant des Bouches du Cattaro," or "Resident of the Bouches du Cattaro," is taken from the collection *Illustrations de L'Illyrie et la Dalmatie,* or *Illustrations of Illyria and Dalmatia,* published in 1815, provided by the Bibliothèque Nationale de France. Each illustration is finely drawn and colored by hand.

In those days, it was easy to identify where people lived and what their trade or station in life was just by their dress. Manning celebrates the inventiveness and initiative of the computer business with book covers based on the rich diversity of regional culture centuries ago, brought back to life by pictures from collections such as this one.

Understanding
generative AI basics

1

This chapter covers

- Introducing generative AI: What's really going on under the hood?
- Distinguishing between the many generative AI models
- Reviewing the global trends that brought about the generative AI revolution

Welcome! As advertised, this book is obsolete, which means that by the time you get around to opening it, most of what's written here will either not work or will be so outdated as to be useless. Now I bet you're feeling just a bit silly for sinking good money into a product like this. Well, I assure you: you don't feel half as weird for buying this book as I felt writing it.

We will definitely get around to the fun stuff—or at least stuff that was fun back in the Before Times when I was originally writing this— soon enough. We'll learn how generative artificial intelligence can be used for far more than just stand-alone ChatGPT prompts. Hopefully, you are curious to learn the answers to the following questions:

- Can AI read statistical data archives and derive serious insights?
- Can AI access the live internet, aggregate data from multiple sites, and use that to pick out real-world trends?
- Can AI accurately summarize large bodies of your own text-based content?
- Can AI models be fine-tuned to provide responses that better match your needs?
- Can AI models be used to generate original video and audio content?

Believe me, I'm also curious. Let's find out.

This book is focused on getting practical stuff done using generative AI tools. That means we're going to minimize some of the under-the-hood theoretical and technical backgrounds that drive these technologies and, instead, concentrate on effective project execution. Expect to learn about new and powerful tools almost immediately and to continue adding skills throughout the rest of the book.

More importantly, expect to become faster and more effective at whatever it is that you do pretty much right away. That's only partly because the large language model (LLM) chat tools like ChatGPT that produce all that generative AI stuff can give you amazing answers to the questions you throw at them. But as you'll see very quickly while working through this book, interacting with LLMs using the automation and scripting tools I'm going to show you will take that to a whole different level.

Nevertheless, I won't lie: you probably won't squeeze every possible drop of AI goodness from your AI prompts without having at least some appreciation for the logic behind moving parts like *models, temperature,* and *text injections*. Every step of every project we'll do here will work and make sense in the context I'll present it. But applying your own customized configurations might be challenging without some technical background, so I've added a full set of definitions in appendix A.

By the way, you can go a long way with these technologies without knowing this, but GPT stands for *Generative Pre-trained Transformer*. Is that important? Not really. However, I will note that the *pre-trained* bit means that we'll be able to enjoy the models even without the need for our own high-end computer hardware.

But first, just what is generative AI, how does it work, and just what is an AI model?

Stepping into the generative AI world

OK, you're in. What's next?

Chatting with a modern AI tool can feel deceptively (Turing test) close to speaking with a real human being. The Turing test is a standard devised by AI pioneer Alan Turing in 1950. A machine was deemed to have achieved the standard of AI if humans could not reliably tell whether they'd just been interacting with another human or a machine.

Well, I can definitely say that had I not knowingly initiated the connection, many of my recent interactions with tools like GPT would have left me unsure of that score. But I did add the word *deceptively* to my description. That's because, in reality, it's all a fake. At this point, at least, even the best AI models aren't actually intelligent in a human way and most certainly aren't aware of their own existence. It's really just clever software combined with massive datasets that give the *impression* of intelligence.

How does that work? The software uses *natural language processing* to analyze the text of your prompt and then, guided by the model's training and configurations, predicts the best possible response. We'll talk more about models in the next chapter. But for now, we'll note that training consists of feeding a model with (pretty much) the entire public internet. All that content is used to analyze human-generated text for patterns so it can use probability calculations to predict the most appropriate way to form its new text.

Initial drafts of a possible response to your specific prompt will be tested against preset standards and preferences and iteratively improved before a final version is displayed for you. If you respond with a follow-up prompt, the LLM will add previous interactions in the session to its context and repeat the process as it works to compose a new response.

As we'll see over and over through the rest of this book, these same processes can be used in a fast-growing range of ways. Beyond text responses, we're already seeing remarkable progress in multi-modal learning, where text prompts can be used to generate audio, images, videos, and who knows what else.

Categorizing AI models by function and objective

Models are the software frameworks that deliver specific features and functionality. For our purposes, the term *model* generally refers to a computational framework designed to understand, generate, or manipulate human language and usually describes LLMs. It learns patterns, semantics, and syntax from vast amounts of text data, enabling it to perform tasks like translation, text generation, and question answering. The LLM's effectiveness relies on its ability to predict and generate coherent sequences of words, making it a versatile tool for natural language understanding and generation across various applications.

An LLM is the engine used to drive a particular provider's product. Thus, OpenAI currently uses GPT-(x), whereas Google's Bard is built on both the Language Model for Dialogue Applications (LaMDA) and the Pathways Language Model 2 (PaLM-2). We're told that PaLM-2 is the LLM that's replacing the LaMDA LLM, which was mostly focused on text-based interactions.

But it's not quite that simple. The very word *model* can have different meanings even within the LLM world. Being clear about this now can help avoid trouble later. For instance, by its own count, OpenAI has seven general-use top-level models, including GPT-3, GPT-3.5, and GPT-4. Just within the context of OpenAI products, the following are some specialized tools also often thought of as models, even though they're actually tapping the functionality of one or another top-level model:

- *DALL-E*—For generating images from text prompts
- *Whisper*—The multilingual speech recognition model
- *The Moderation model*—Designed specifically to optimize measuring compliance with OpenAI usage policies to help ensure an LLM isn't misused
- *Embeddings*—A classification tool for measuring the relatedness between two pieces of text, a key element in the work LLMs do
- *Codex*—The engine driving the programming assistant used by Copilot, GitHub's AI tool for generating contextually-aware programming code

But those shouldn't be confused with the long list of GPT model flavors available to choose from, such as `code-davinci-002` and `gpt-3.5-turbo`. For some reason, OpenAI (https://platform .openai.com/docs/models/gpt-3-5) also refers to each of those as models. While you're not wrong for calling them *models*, it might be a bit more accurate to describe them as specialized *versions* of a top-level GPT model.

Whatever you prefer to call them, it'll be useful to know how they work. So let's take a look at each of the (currently) active models you can select for your operations. Even if the precise names listed here might be different from what you'll probably see on official sites way off in the deep, distant future of, I don't know, next Thursday, being familiar with these will still provide useful background.

Understanding usage tokens

It can be helpful to think of a token as a unit of language characters. Within the GPT universe at least, one token is more or less equal to four characters of English text. Sometimes we're interested in how many tokens a task will consume and, other times, on what kinds of tokens will do the best job completing a task. The most obvious differences between various model flavors are their maximum token limits and the cutoff date for their training data. You're generally billed according the number of such units a prompt consumes.

Models based on GPT-3, for example, were trained only on data in existence up to September 2021. And they won't allow a single request to consume more than 2,049 tokens between both the prompt and completion (i.e., response). By contrast, the newer GPT-4 Turbo model has knowledge of world events up to April 2023 and offers what they call a 128k context window. A context window reflects the range of text that the model considers when processing or generating language. Those limits will affect how much content you can incorporate into your prompts and how much depth you can expect from the responses.

A limit of 2,049 tokens, for example, means that total content of both your prompt and its response cannot use up more than around 1,600 words. So if your prompt is, say, already 1,000 words long, there won't be much space left for a response. As we'll see later, however, there are various tools available for circumventing at least some token limits for any model.

GPT-4 models

There are currently two models within the GPT-4 family: GPT-4 and GPT-4 Turbo. At least as of my getting out of bed this morning, GPT-4 was still not fully available across all platforms. Also, the laundry basket was sticking out, and I bumped into it on my way to the bathroom.

GPT-3.5 models

There are four long-term models based on GPT-3.5. All but `code-davinci-002` allow 4,097 tokens. A single `code-davinci-002` prompt/completion can consume as many as 8,001 tokens. Let's describe each of those models:

- `gpt-3.5-turbo-instruct` combines the ability to follow instructions found in the older `text-davinci` series with the kinds of performance speeds as newer turbo models.
- `gpt-3.5-turbo` is optimized for chat (of the ChatGPT type), although it's still a good general-purpose model, and it's both more capable and significantly cheaper than other GPT-3.5 models.

- `text-davinci-003` is technically a legacy model and is focused on language-based tasks and has been optimized for *consistent instruction-following*. This refers to the ability of a language model to consistently and accurately follow a set of instructions provided by a user or a prompt. This model has been largely replaced by the newer `gpt-3.5-turbo-instruct`.
- `text-davinci-002` is comparable to `text-davinci-003`, but it was trained using supervised fine-tuning, which is a machine learning technique used to improve the performance of a pre-trained model to adapt it to perform specific tasks or to make it more useful for particular applications.
- `code-davinci-002` is primarily optimized for tasks involving programming code completion to help users solve programming problems.

GPT-3 models

As I'm sure you've noticed, OpenAI uses the names of great innovators in science and technology when naming its models. That's nowhere more obvious than in the names they use for GPT-3:

- `text-curie-001` is described as capable while being particularly inexpensive.
- `text-babbage-001` is perhaps not as much of a general-purpose tool but, for text classifications, it excels. That could include determine the sentiment (positive, negative, neutral) of customer reviews or social media posts. This is known as *sentiment analysis*.
- `text-ada-001` is, for most purposes, extremely fast, and it's most effective at simple natural language tasks like conversation.
- `davinci` is an excellent general-purpose model capable of handling more complicated text processing to better understand the nuances of human language.
- `curie` is both faster and cheaper than `davinci`.

- `babbage` is described in identical terms to `text-babbage-001`, although its capacity of 125 million parameters is far lower than the 1.2 billion parameters of `text-babbage-001`.
- `ada` is described in identical terms to `ada-001`, but similar to `babbage`, its capacity (40 million parameters) is far lower than that of `text-ada-001` (125 million parameters).

Training parameters

Incorporating more parameters into the training of an LLM enhances its capacity to capture intricate language patterns and knowledge, resulting in improved performance. The larger the model size, the better understanding of contex and the finer-grained text generation you'll get. So if "bigger is better," why don't all models use 10 billions parameters? That's because it would require substantial computational resources, data, and costs to train effectively.

If the distinctions between all of those model use cases feels a bit abstract, don't worry. In fact, all existing models are probably going to do a decent job on nearly everything you throw at them. The important thing is to know that specializations exist and that you may need to seek out the right one should you ever have a particularly cutting-edge need.

Model fine-tuning

Fine-tuning refers to the process of further training a pretrained language model on specific tasks or domains using labeled data or prompts. The objective of fine-tuning is to adapt the pretrained model to a particular task, making it more specialized and capable of generating more accurate and contextually relevant responses. Fine-tuning *can* be part of the ChatGPT prompt creation process. However, the fine-tuned big picture extends well beyond simple prompts to encompass much more sophisticated configurations of AI models. Following are the steps that can be used through the entire process:

- *Pretraining*—A language model is initially trained on a large corpus of text data to learn general language patterns, grammar, and semantic representations. This pretraining phase allows the model to develop a broad understanding of language and acquire knowledge about various domains and topics.
- *Task-specific dataset*—To fine-tune the pretrained model for a specific task, a labeled dataset or prompts related to that task are required. The dataset contains examples or prompts paired with the desired outputs or correct responses. For example, in sentiment analysis, the dataset would consist of sentences labeled as positive or negative sentiments.
- *Architecture adaptation*—The pretrained language model's architecture is usually modified or extended to accommodate the specific task or requirements. This may involve adding task-specific layers, modifying the model's attention mechanisms, or adjusting the output layers to match the desired task format.
- *Fine-tuning process*—The pretrained model is then further trained on the task-specific dataset or prompts. During fine-tuning, the model's parameters are updated using gradient-based optimization algorithms, such as stochastic gradient descent (SGD) or Adam to minimize the difference between the model's predictions and the desired outputs in the labeled dataset. This process allows the model to specialize and adapt its representations to the specific task at hand.
- *Iterative refinement*—Fine-tuning is typically an iterative process. The model is trained on the task-specific dataset for multiple epochs, adjusting the parameters and optimizing the model's performance over time. The fine-tuning process aims to improve the model's accuracy and contextual understanding and generate task-specific responses.

By fine-tuning a pretrained language model, the model can use its general language understanding and adapt it to perform more effectively and accurately on specific tasks or domains. This approach saves significant computational resources and training time compared to training a model from scratch. Fine-tuning allows for task specialization and enables the model to generate contextually relevant responses based on the specific prompts or tasks it has been trained on.

The technologies that make generative AI work

I could spend pages and pages describing the key software frameworks and methodologies that fueled the AI explosion. In fact, you can find those very pages in the appendix A, as previously mentioned. But those represent ideas and often decades-old ideas at that. What's been holding those ideas back all this time? It's not like there weren't crowds of extremely smart engineers, mathematicians, and theoretical researchers working on the problem back in the 1970s, 1980s, 1990s, and 2000s. And it's not like there weren't hyperambitious tech entrepreneurs aggressively looking for the Next Big Thing back then. What prevented all this from happening 30 or even 10 years ago?

Most of the bottleneck was due to hardware limitations. For those of you old enough to remember, the costs and physical constraints of processor speeds, disk storage, and volatile memory made for a very different computing experience in, say, 1990. That was when I got my first work computer, a hand-me-down from a business that had, until just before, been using it for cutting-edge scientific research. That monster boasted a whopping 640k of RAM, a 10 MB hard drive, and a text-only display. Video graphics memory? Don't make me laugh. Its CPU didn't even have a math co-processor.

The workstation I'm currently using has more than 20,000 times more memory and 5,000 times more storage space. And it cost me 1/4 of 1 percent of the price (when adjusted for inflation). I'm sure you get the picture. Without cheap storage, memory, processors, and especially graphics processing units (GPUs) and tensor processing unit (TPUs), it would have been simply impossible to imagine training and then deploying the original pioneering LLMs like GPT.

Beyond that, the easy availability of all those resources in a production-ready state on cloud platforms—specifically, Microsoft's Azure—probably cut years off development times. From my early career in IT, I know how long it takes to research, tender bids, seek approval, purchase, wait for delivery, and then actually deploy hardware on-premises. And that was for one or two rack servers or network switches at a time. I can barely fathom what it would have taken to put together the kind of hardware necessary to drive GPT development. But with the cloud, it's really only a matter of entering your credit card information and clicking a few buttons.

Besides the actual hardware infrastructure, there were three other critical trends that made modern AI possible:

- *Access to large-scale datasets (i.e., the internet)*—The existence of vast amounts of labeled (for example, data or images that have been tagged with verified descriptions) and unlabeled data, often referred to as big data, facilitated the training of generative AI models by providing a diverse and representative sample of real-world examples.
- *Increased computational efficiency*—Optimization techniques, such as parallel processing, distributed computing, and model compression, played a crucial role in improving the efficiency of generative AI models, making them more practical and feasible for real-world applications.
- *Research collaborations and knowledge sharing*—The active collaboration and exchange of ideas within the research community accelerated progress in generative AI, enabling the cross-pollination of techniques, methodologies, and best practices.

And finally, there's Moore's law—an observation and prediction made by Gordon Moore, co-founder of Intel, in 1965. It states that the number of transistors on a microchip doubles approximately every two years, leading to a significant increase in computing power while reducing costs. In other words, the density of transistors on integrated circuits tends to double every 18 to 24 months. This exponential growth in transistor count has been a driving force behind the rapid advancement of technology, enabling more powerful and efficient computers, as well as smaller and more capable electronic devices. Although Moore's law is not a physical law, it has held true for several decades and has guided the semiconductor industry's progress.

AI and data privacy and ownership

Throughout this book, we're going to be using all kinds of generative AI tools in all kinds of ways. And when I say "using generative AI tools," I really mean exposing your prompts and, in many cases, data resources to online services. This can raise concerns about the collection and use of personal data, particularly if the data is sensitive or contains personally identifiable information (PII). It is important to understand how the AI is collecting and using data and to only provide data that is necessary and appropriate for the intended purpose.

Some AI tools may monitor user activity and collect information about users' interactions with the technology. This could potentially raise concerns about surveillance and the misuse of personal information. Users should be aware of what information is being collected and how it will be used before engaging with an AI.

Publicly available generative AIs may also pose security risks if they are not properly secured. For example, if an attacker gains access to an AI's training data or model architecture, they could potentially use this information to launch targeted attacks against users (meaning *you*). There may be risks associated with integrating LLMs into critical infrastructure systems, such as power grids or financial networks. So if you work in—oh, I don't know—a nuclear weapons facility, you should perhaps think carefully before introducing GPT around the office.

Hoping for the best is always an excellent approach. But it's probably also a good idea to at least think about security and privacy concerns. Consider the following best practices:

- Choose AI tools from reputable developers who have a track record of prioritizing privacy and ethics.
- Review the tools' documentation and terms of service to understand how they collect, use, and protect user data.

- Get in the habit of only providing data that's necessary and appropriate for the intended purpose.
- Protect your own programming code and infrastructure from unauthorized access and exploitation.

From the other side, you should also consider how, through your use of generative AI services, you might be stepping on someone else's rights. It's unlikely, but an AI might produce text that's uncomfortably similar to content it was trained on. If any of that content was not in the public domain or available rights-free, you might end up publishing some else's protected property as your own. We call that *plagiarism.*

Having said that, out of curiosity I once asked a friend to submit a very large body of text from GPT to a professional plagiarism detecting service to see what came back. Not a single one of the tens of thousands of AI-generated words in the sample was identified as a problem. So the odds are you'll possibly never encounter this kind of trouble in the real world. Having said that, you'll see a nasty, real-world counterexample for yourself when you get to chapter 3. So it can't hurt to be just a little bit paranoid. Better safe than sorry.

AI and reliability

We should also share a word or two about *hallucinations.* Although before we begin, you might want to make sure GPT (and friends) aren't within earshot. From experience, I can tell you that they don't react well to these discussions.

Put bluntly, AIs will sometimes produce output that qualifies more as creative than clever. They've been caught inventing legal precedents, academic papers, authors, and even entire universities. To put that in context, I had a high school student who would sometimes do all that too. But he was just cheerfully pranking the system to see whether anyone would notice. And he went on to a successful academic and professional career. Your friendly LLM, by contrast, has no clue that there's anything wrong at all and will often politely suggest that this is all your fault ("I apologize for the confusion . . .").

Similarly, AIs are generally no better than the content they've been fed. While OpenAI and other AI companies have tried to minimize the problem, there is some evidence that LLMs will sometimes adopt the subjective political or social opinions of their training content and appear to take sides on controversial topics. This, too, should be a consideration when consuming AI responses.

LLMs are also notoriously bad at simple arithmetic. I recently fed a PDF file containing historical sales data for books to an AI. Some individual titles had more than one entry, representing multiple editions of the same book, in the file. I thought I'd save myself 5 or 10 minutes of work setting up a simple spreadsheet by having the AI do the calculations.

Here was my prompt:

 Based on the PDF, can you tell me how many copies of each title were sold in total. I'd like you to ignore individual ISBN numbers and just look at the book titles.

No matter how often and precisely I rephrased that prompt, the AI insisted on picking one value seemingly at random, ignoring all the others, and presenting that single number as the total. But it was unfailingly polite:

 I apologize for the confusion. You are correct that I missed some entries in my previous responses. Here are the corrected total net units sold for each book title, taking into account all entries in the PDF.

The lesson is that we should treat LLMs the way journalists are supposed to treat sources: "If your mother says she loves you, demand corroboration." In other words, check facts and sources yourself before publishing AI output.

What's still ahead?

Before moving on, I'd like to let you in on the big picture. Here's what we're planning to cover:

- Customizing text, code, and media content creation based on your organization's data and specific needs

- Training AI models on your local data stores or on the live internet
- Discovering business intelligence and analytics applications for AI
- Building your own AI models
- Looking ahead to the future of generative AI

It just gets crazier from here.

That's how things look from this end. Now get reading. I'll see you on the other side.

Summary

- Generative AI is built on dozens of tools, methodologies, and technologies, including natural language processing, reinforcement learning, and neural networks.
- Technological advances in data storage, graphics processing, and network connectivty, along with steady reductions in hardware costs, have contributed to the generative AI revolution.

Managing
generative AI

This chapter covers

- Understanding how to access and interact with AI models in the most productive ways possible
- Configuring models to provide the best fit possible for your specific needs
- Using the OpenAI Playground to better understand key tools for controlling AI

Throwing clever prompts at an AI chat interface can definitely produce impressive results. But by ignoring the finer points of model configuration, you'll be missing out on most of your AI's potential value. So with this chapter, we'll begin the process of figuring out which dials to turn and how far to turn them (and which big red button you should absolutely avoid).

Of course, for all I know, by the time you get around to reading this, the whole process might be automated. That blue light gently pulsing on your keyboard that you can't resist staring at? That would be the brainwave scanner GPT now uses to directly download your innermost goals and desires. Your results are available now.

Accessing GPT models

In case you haven't yet had the pleasure, most popular interactive AI platforms require you to create an account before trying them out. For OpenAI's ChatGPT, that'll happen at https://chat.openai .com/auth/login. Even if you're asked to provide credit card information, you'll be given plenty of warning before you're actually billed. Just don't ignore those warnings.

Once you're signed up, the ChatGPT interface is available at https://chat.openai.com/.

Now what? Besides ChatGPT, it doesn't require a PhD in electrical engineering to realize that Microsoft's Bing search engine gives you access to GPT-4 from within the Edge browser. I'd mention Google's GPT competitor, Gemini here, too. But Gemini hasn't had an easy childhood so far. You can expect to come across all kinds of geographic, commercial, or even technological restrictions on how and when you can access various AI services as they evolve. Anthropic's Claude (https://claude.ai/) is another good example. Be patient and flexible.

> **NOTE** I should also tell you about ChatGPT Plus, which is OpenAI's subscription-only version of ChatGPT. The Plus service offers multimodel integration with, for instance, image and plot generation and at least partial access to the live internet. Plus will cost you around $20 a month, but that can be a smart investment for certain business needs. Nevertheless, none of the use cases we'll discuss in this book will require a Plus subscription.

Besides those web services that are hosted directly by their creators, there are also plenty of third-party web projects, such as ChatPDF (https://www.chatpdf.com/) for analyzing PDF documents and

Rytr (https://rytr.me) for generating written content, that offer nice managed applications for specialized use cases. There's nothing particularly complicated about putting those to use, either. We will talk more about those kinds of services later.

But all that's consumer-quality stuff. It's OK. But the serious work, you might say, is happening "off-campus"—meaning high-productivity interactions, like carefully configuring your model, letting your AI loose on large stores of your own data, or automating multiple rounds of prompts and completions and then incorporating the responses into your code-driven workflow.

No matter which models you're using, this kind of access will happen through an application programming interface (API). As illustrated in figure 2.1, an API serves as a bridge between software applications, allowing them to communicate and interact. It defines a set of rules and protocols that enable one application to request services or data from another. APIs provide developers with the appropriate authorization to access a service's specific functionalities. They enable seamless integration by specifying how requests should be structured and how responses will be formatted.

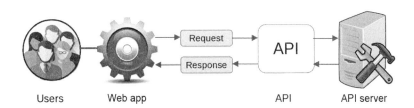

Figure 2.1.   A typical API architecture

A lot of the technical examples you'll see later in the book will happen through APIs. For practical reasons, those will mostly use OpenAI models and infrastructure. But the broad underlying methodologies should mostly apply to other services too (once they become widely available).

So the road to coding your AI leads through APIs. But don't worry if you've never done this kind of thing before. I'll give you all the background and technical details you'll need to make everything work just fine. Just keep in mind that API requests are usually subject to charges. Individual interactions will incur fractions of pennies each, but once you incorporate API calls into programmed automations, the costs can start to climb. Before we go there, though, we should check out OpenAI's Playground (https://platform.openai .com/playground).

Learning by playing

The Playground, shown in figure 2.2, existed even before ChatGPT, and it was where I had my first interactions with GPT. However, keep in mind that, along with everything else in the AI world, the interface will probably have changed at least twice by the time you get to it. We're going to use the Playground throughout this chapter to learn how to interact with GPT.

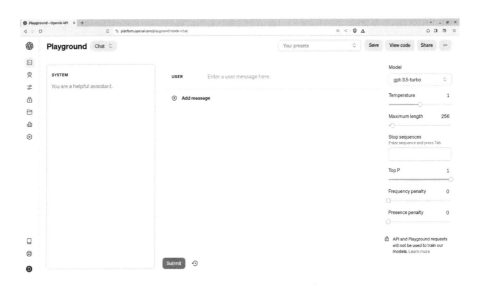

Figure 2.2.   OpenAI's Playground interface

You get to the Playground from your OpenAI login account. Rather than enjoying a sustained conversation where subsequent exchanges are informed by earlier prompts and completions, when the Chat option is selected from the pull-down menu at the top-left of the screen, the text field in the Playground offers only one exchange at a time. The models it's based on might also be a bit older and less refined than the ChatGPT version.

But there are two things that set the Playground apart from ChatGPT. One is the configuration controls displayed down the right side of the screen in figure 2.2, and the second is the View Code feature at the top-right. Those features make the Playground primarily an educational tool rather than just another GPT interface.

Accessing Python code samples

We're going to look at those features one at a time in the next section of this chapter. But, accessing the GPT API using code will probably give you the greatest value over the long term. I really want to show you what View Code is all about right away. Figure 2.3 shows a typical Playground session where I've typed in a prompt and then clicked the View Code button with the Python option selected. I'm shown the working code, which, assuming you'll add a valid OpenAI API key on line 4, can be copied and run from any internet-connected computer.

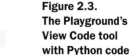

View code

You can use the following code to start integrating your current prompt and settings into your application.

```
POST /v1/completions                                python ⌄   ⧉ Copy

1   import os
2   import openai
3
4   openai.api_key = os.getenv("OPENAI_API_KEY")
5
6   response = openai.Completion.create(
7       model="text-davinci-003",
8       prompt="Explain the purpose of Temperature as a configuration tool i
9       temperature=
10      max_tokens=
11      top_p=,
12      frequency_penalty=,
13      presence_penalty=
14  )
```

Your API Key can be found here. You should use environment variables or a secret management tool to expose your key to your applications.

Close

**Figure 2.3.
The Playground's
View Code tool
with Python code**

Don't worry about the details right now, but take a moment to look through the arguments included in the `openai.Completion` `.create()` method. The model that's currently selected in the Model field on the right side of the Playground is there (`text` `-davinci-003`), as is my actual prompt (`Explain the purpose` `of . . .`). In fact, each configuration option I've selected is there. In other words, I can experiment with any combination of configurations here in the Playground and then copy the code and run it, or variations of it, anywhere. This, in fact, is where you learn how to use the API.

Accessing curl code samples

Figure 2.4 shows us how that exact same prompt would work if I decided to use the command line tool, `curl`, instead of Python. Besides Python and curl, you can also display code in node.js and JSON.

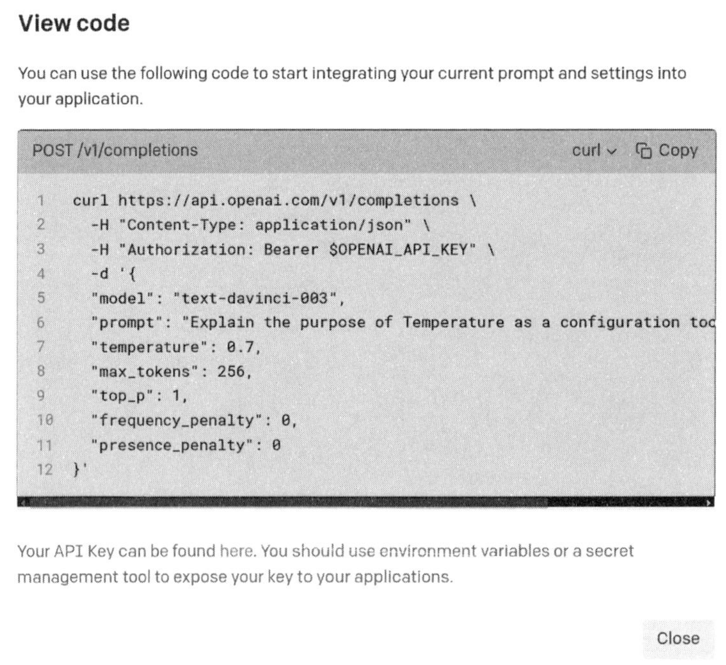

View code

You can use the following code to start integrating your current prompt and settings into your application.

```
POST /v1/completions                                     curl ∨   ⎘ Copy

  1   curl https://api.openai.com/v1/completions \
  2      -H "Content-Type: application/json" \
  3      -H "Authorization: Bearer $OPENAI_API_KEY" \
  4      -d '{
  5      "model": "text-davinci-003",
  6      "prompt": "Explain the purpose of Temperature as a configuration too
  7      "temperature": 0.7,
  8      "max_tokens": 256,
  9      "top_p": 1,
 10      "frequency_penalty": 0,
 11      "presence_penalty": 0
 12   }'
```

Your API Key can be found here. You should use environment variables or a secret management tool to expose your key to your applications.

Close

Figure 2.4.   The Playground's View Code tool with `curl` code

> **NOTE** `curl` is a venerable open source command line tool
> that's often available by default. To confirm it's available on your
> system, simply type `curl` at any command-line prompt. You
> should see some kind of help message with suggestions for
> proper usage.

One more thing: table 2.1 shows each available OpenAI model, along with its associated API endpoints. An endpoint is an address that can be used within your code to access a resource. Besides the value of having that information, endpoints are also important because they show us the kinds of prompts you can send. Besides the `completions` operations that you'd expect, there are also `edits`, `transcriptions`, `translations`, `fine-tunes`, `embeddings`, and `moderations`. We'll talk more about using those later in the book. But do keep them all in mind.

Table 2.1. OpenAI models and endpoints

Endpoint	Model name
`/v1/chat/completions`	`GPT-4 Turbo, gpt-4, gpt-4-0314, gpt-4-32k, gpt-4-32k-0314, gpt-3.5-turbo, gpt-3.5-turbo-0301`
`/v1/completions`	`text-davinci-003, text-davinci-002, text-curie-001, text-babbage-001, text-ada-001`
`/v1/edits`	`text-davinci-edit-001, code-davinci-edit-001`
`/v1/audio/transcriptions`	`whisper-1`
`/v1/audio/translations`	`whisper-1`
`/v1/fine-tunes`	`davinci, curie, babbage, ada`
`/v1/embeddings`	`text-embedding-ada-002, text-search-ada-doc-001`
`/v1/moderations`	`text-moderation-stable, text-moderation-latest`

> **TIP** No matter which AI you're using, make sure you understand
> all available options so you can optimize your environment.

Completion configurations

You could think of completion configurations as a kind of fine-tuning, and you wouldn't be wrong. However, in the context of AI, the term *fine-tuning* can have far more specific meanings. We'll spend more time discussing that topic in chapters 6 and 9. Before I start explaining how each of these configurations works, let's look at figure 2.5, which should help you visualize what an AI model might do to your prompt before spitting out a response.

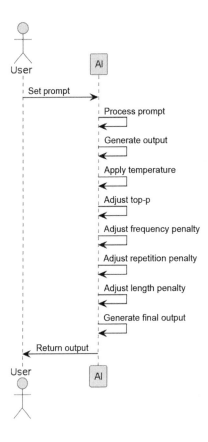

Figure 2.5. How parameters are applied to an AI prompt

As you can see, a typical language model (LM) might immediately produce a tentative draft response (in the diagram, Generate Output). But, before sharing it with you (Return Output), it'll first test it for compliance with any preferences (i.e., temperature, frequency, and so on) you might have set. Those preferences, which we'll soon see in action, can control a prompt's tone, creativity, focus, verbosity, and even cost. Figure 2.6 shows what those controls look like in the Playground.

Figure 2.6. **Upper selection of tools in the Playground UI**

Now let's see what those are really all about. Just to keep you oriented, we'll cover each of these configuration categories:

- Mode
- Temperature
- Top P value
- Stop sequences
- Frequency penalty

- Presence penalty
- Best of
- Inject start text

To give you some context, imagine you're building a web application that provides on-demand responses to user questions about your hotel. You might initially ask your users to select from a list of categories ("dining and entertainment," "trip planning," and so on). Based on the category they choose, you want to fine-tune your chat tool so that the responses are a good match for the users' expectations. These configurations can help you create just such an customization.

Setting the mode

Depending on the model you're using, the Mode drop-down might have three options: Chat, Complete, and Edit. Complete and Chat provide the familiar completion and chat experiences we're already used to. If you have some text you'd like to rework in one way or another, you can select the Edit mode and enter your text in the Input section and what you'd like changed in the text in the Instructions field. The Playground suggests "Fix the grammar" as a possible instruction, but you're free to use your own. We'll learn more about this kind of operation in the next chapter.

The prebuilt list in the Model drop-down displays all the OpenAI models available for the currently selected mode. This list will change dynamically based on the mode you've selected. You'll obviously want to select a model that's the best fit for your needs and budget (as described in the following discussion).

Setting the temperature

Temperature controls the amount of randomness used in the generation of output. It allows the user to adjust the level of creativity and unpredictability in the output. By setting the temperature to a value between 0 and 2 (the default is 1), the AI can generate different types of output, ranging from highly creative and unpredictable (i.e., 2) to highly structured and conservative (i.e,. 0).

Let's consider an example using a chatbot scenario where a user asks for a restaurant recommendation:

 Can you suggest a good restaurant nearby?

We can use different temperature settings to generate responses with varying degrees of randomness. A higher temperature (e.g., 1.3) encourages the LM to produce more diverse and creative responses, even if they might be less focused or accurate:

 Sure! How about trying the cozy little café around the corner? They serve delicious food, from gourmet burgers to exotic sushi. You'll definitely have an adventurous dining experience there!

In this case, the high-temperature setting led to a more imaginative response, suggesting a variety of food options and emphasizing an "adventurous dining experience."

On the other hand, a lower temperature (e.g., 0.2) encourages the LM to produce more deterministic and focused responses, often sticking to safe and conventional choices:

 Sure! I recommend the Italian restaurant on Main Street. They have authentic pasta dishes and mouthwatering pizzas. You won't be disappointed!

With the lower temperature, the response is more straightforward and focuses on a specific cuisine and establishment, providing a safe and reliable recommendation.

Setting the Top P value

Top P (also known as nucleus sampling or penalty-free sampling) is a parameter that helps control the diversity of the generated text. It involves selecting the most likely words for the next token in a sequence, considering a cumulative probability threshold (P). Instead of generating from its entire vocabulary, it narrows choices to a subset of the most probable words whose cumulative probabilities exceed P. This helps control the output's length and diversity while maintaining coherence.

When using the Top P sampling approach, the model selects the most likely next word based on a probability threshold (p), which allows for more diverse and controlled output. Words with cumulative probabilities that exceed the threshold are considered, ensuring a balance between predictability and creativity in the generated text. In simpler terms, Top P allows the model to think beyond the obvious choices while still staying coherent. It's like giving the AI a bit of freedom to surprise you while ensuring the generated text remains meaningful. This technique is particularly useful when you want creative responses that don't completely deviate from the topic.

By adjusting the Top P value, users can influence the amount of randomness or diversity in the model's responses. A higher value (e.g., `0.9`) includes a larger set of potential tokens, making the output more diverse, while a lower value (e.g., `0.1`) narrows the choices, resulting in more focused and deterministic outputs. The default Top P value is `1`.

The following is an example where a user asks for information about the weather:

 What's the weather like today?

Naturally, that'll only work with models with access to real-time data sources. We can explore the effect of different Top P values on the response generation. Here is the response with the Top P value of `0.2` (highly focused):

 The weather today is sunny with a high of 25 degrees Celsius. It's a perfect day to enjoy outdoor activities.

With a low Top P value, the model selects only the most likely next words, resulting in focused and deterministic responses that are generally more reliable but less varied:

 Today's weather is sunny, warm, and delightful. You might want to grab your sunglasses and head out for a fun-filled day!

With a higher Top P value of `0.8` (more diverse), the model considers a broader range of likely next words, resulting in more diverse responses. This can introduce variations in the generated text, offering different ways of expressing the same information.

While Top P and temperature seem similar, temperature controls the randomness in language generation: higher values (e.g., 1.0) increase diversity, and lower values (e.g., 0.2) produce more predictable output. By contrast, Top P sampling sets a probability threshold (p) to select from a subset of the most probable words, adjusting output diversity based on the threshold (e.g., p = 0.9 for more diversity; p = 0.2 for less diversity). As a rule, one can alter Temperature or Top P but not both.

Working with stop sequences

Stop sequences are special tokens used to indicate the end of a generated response or to prompt the model to stop generating further text. These tokens are typically added to the input prompt to control the length of the generated output.

In English, a common example of an end-of-sentence token is the period (.), followed by a space. In programming languages, a common stop sequence might be a pair of curly braces ({}) to indicate the end of a code block. In HTML or XML, a closing tag like `</tag>` signals the end of an element.

It's important to note that modern MLs like GPT do not necessarily rely on explicit stop sequences to generate text. Instead, they often use techniques like tokenization and context windows to understand where to naturally conclude sentences or paragraphs. Additionally, they may use special tokens like `<eos>` (end of sequence) internally, but these details are typically abstracted away from the user.

For instance, in the middle of explaining a lesson, a virtual instructor could be configured to say, "Let's stop here for today. Repeat back to me the three main points of this lesson." After the student responds with the three main points (matching the required stop sequence), the instructor could say, "Yes, excellent! Alright, that concludes our session today."

Setting the frequency penalty

The frequency penalty is used to discourage repetitive or redundant output. It helps address a common issue where models tend to produce repetitive or excessively long phrases, leading to less coherent and less diverse responses. By applying a frequency penalty, users can control the tradeoff between generating diverse responses and avoiding repetitive patterns.

The penalty is calculated based on the number of times a generated token or sequence of tokens has already appeared in the output. When the penalty is applied, the model's probability distribution over tokens is adjusted to decrease the likelihood of generating tokens that have already been used. The purpose of the frequency penalty is to encourage the model to explore alternative options and generate more varied and coherent responses.

The penalty value, which can lie between `-2.0` and `2.0`, can be adjusted based on the desired level of repetition avoidance. Higher penalty values result in stronger discouragement of repetition, while lower values allow for more flexibility in the generated output. Finding the right balance is important to ensure the generated text remains coherent and contextually relevant while avoiding excessive repetition. Consider the following example where a user asks for some ideas for a new smartphone:

🔘 **DA** Generate some ideas for a new smartphone.

🌀 Sure! Here are a few ideas: a high-resolution display, multiple camera lenses, fast processing speed, long battery life, and a sleek design.

That LM generated ideas that are already common—it's hardly ground breaking. However, you can add a frequency penalty.

🔘 **DA** Generate some ideas for a new smartphone while using a frequency penalty to encourage unique and rare features.

🌀 Certainly! How about a smartphone with a holographic display that projects 3D images, a graphene-based battery for instant charging, a customizable modular design allowing users to swap hardware

components, a built-in AI language translator for real-time conversations, and a biometric authentication system that reads unique vein
patterns in the user's palm?

In this case, by using a frequency penalty, the model is more likely
to generate ideas that involve less common words or concepts. This
results in suggestions that are more innovative and imaginative,
aligning with your goal of coming up with unique product features.

Setting the presence penalty

The presence penalty is a parameter in GPT models that helps control the repetition of phrases and words in the generated text. It's
designed to prevent the model from repeating the same phrases
or words too often in the generated output. The presence penalty
modifies the probability distribution so that the use of words in the
input prompt or seed text is less likely. This encourages the model
to generate words and cover topics that were not explicit in the
input.

Although the presence and frequency penalties do seem to over-
lap, they're not identical. The frequency penalty is a contribution
that is proportional to how often a specific token has already been
sampled. It discourages the model from repeating the same words
or phrases too frequently within the generated text. On the other
hand, the presence penalty is a one-time, additive contribution
that applies to all tokens that have been sampled at least once. It
modifies the probability distribution so that it's less likely that the
response will include words used in the input prompt or seed text.
This encourages the model to generate words that were not in the
input.

We can explore the effect of different presence penalty values on
the response generation while comparing it with the frequency penalty. Imagine you prompted the model: "Tell me about the recent
performance of my favorite sports team." Here is the response with
the presence penalty value set at 0.2 (less avoidance):

Your favorite sports team has been performing exceptionally well in recent matches. They have displayed remarkable teamwork and strategic play, leading to several victories.

With a lower presence penalty, the model may generate responses that contain the desired keywords or concepts more frequently, as it is less inclined to avoid using them. Doing the same thing with the frequency penalty set at 0.2 (less repetition), on the other hand, would produce the following response.

 Your favorite sports team has had an impressive run in recent games. They showcased great skill, coordination, and game-changing strategies, resulting in a string of successes.

In comparison to presence penalty, the frequency penalty focuses on reducing the repetition of specific phrases or responses, irrespective of their relevance to the user's input.

By adjusting the presence penalty, you can control how much the AI adheres to specific keywords or concepts in its generated text. Lower values may result in the model mentioning the desired topics more frequently, while higher values encourage the model to avoid excessive repetition of those topics.

The following is an example of how you might use a high presence penalty in an LM prompt. Imagine that you're using an LM to generate a story or conversation, and you want to ensure that the generated text avoids any mention of violence or graphic content. You want to apply a high presence penalty to ensure that the model strictly avoids using words or phrases related to violence.

 Create a story about two adventurers on a quest to save their kingdom from a great threat. Apply a high presence penalty to avoid any description of violence or graphic scenes.

By using a high presence penalty, you can guide the LM to generate responses that adhere to specific content guidelines, making it suitable for various contexts where certain topics or language need to be avoided.

Besides the configuration controls that you can see on the Playground page, there are some other controls that are both fairly common and useful.

Working with Best Of

When generating responses from a generative AI model, you may sometimes receive multiple candidate outputs. The Best Of approach involves selecting the most suitable or highest-quality response from these candidates based on certain criteria. The default setting (1) will stream all outputs without any selection or filtering. Higher values (up to 20) will increase the ratio of possibility generations to outputs that you're shown.

The purpose of the Best Of approach is to curate and refine the output by handpicking the most favorable response among several options. It allows you to have more control over the final output, ensuring it meets your desired standards or aligns with the intended purpose of the generative AI model. But keep in mind: the higher the Best Of value, the more you pay for each output.

For example, in a text summarization task, you may want to identify the most important phrases or sentences that capture the essence of a document or article. You could use `best of` to extract the top n phrases or sentences based on their importance or relevance and then use these phrases to generate a summary of the original text.

Working with the Inject Start Text setting

The Inject Start Text or Input Prefix setting guides or conditions the model's output based on specific initial text provided by the user. It involves prepending or inserting a prompt, question, or context at the beginning of the input sequence to influence the generated response. By injecting start text, you can provide the model with additional context or information that helps steer its output in a desired direction. Unlike the other prompt tools we've seen, the Injected Start Text setting becomes an integral part of the input prompt itself and serves as the beginning of the generated response. This can be useful in scenarios where you want the generated text to be more focused, specific, or tailored to a particular context.

For example, if you are using an LM to generate responses in a customer support chatbot, you can inject start text such as "User: What is the return policy for your products?" before the model generates a response. This helps frame the conversation and ensures the model understands the context of the user's query. Rather than specifying text to prefix a completion, `inject restart text` allows users to continue a patterned conversation structure by inserting text within a completion.

There are, as you might imagine, many more cool and wonderful things you can do with GPT via the API. We'll certainly be touching on many of them throughout the rest of this book. You can (and should) visit the API reference page (https://platform.openai .com/docs/api-reference/authentication) early and often.

> **TIP** Any generative AI operation that's more complicated than a simple request for information—and certainly any automated prompt delivered programmatically—can probably be executed more effectively by tweaking your model's parameters. So consider moving beyond the default settings for things like frequency and temperature.

And I'm supposed to understand how all this stuff works?

Summary

- There are multiple classes of generative AI model, including software frameworks like GPT and PaLM-2 and more specific task-based modules like GPT's `davinci` and `ada`. Each has its own best-use scenarios.

- OpenAI's Playground is a valuable tool for learning about the configuration options GPT offers and generating code for running prompts programmatically. You should use the Playground as a source for custom-built code for executing prompts through the OpenAI API.

- Configuration controls, like temperature, presence penalties, and Best Of can be used to fine-tune your model prompts. There are generally interactive tools for applying these controls no matter which AI model you're using.

- The OpenAI API reference guide (https://platform.openai .com/docs/api-reference) is an important resource. Make it your best friend.

- We explored fine-tuning in its larger context, giving us a quick glimpse into some of the flexibility that's possible with large LMs.

Creating text and code

This chapter covers

- Automating the process of filtering content for accuracy
- Creating new content based on complex details you can define
- Generating customized documentation matching specialized fields
- Generating programming code

Until now we've explored some of the underlying context and mechanics of generative AI: how it works and how you can fine-tune it. Beginning with this chapter, we'll be working with some actual content generation.

But how exactly is that going to work? Well, I don't see much point in me throwing you a long list of ChatGPT prompts. I'm sure you've already done plenty of that. And in case you haven't, typing "cool prompts for ChatGPT" into your favorite internet search engine will soon fix you up.

What I am going to give you is some more complex and sometimes unexpected approaches to dealing with bigger problems, including how to train your AI model to work within a closely defined conceptual universe and how to build real-world websites just by describing them. We're going to use all the same toys everyone else is playing with, but we're going to be tweaking things to better fit our specific needs.

> **NOTE** One caveat. As I'll point out more than once in the coming chapters, I don't expect you to use the tricks and configurations we'll encounter exactly the way I'm presenting them. Rather, the goal is to provide some basic skills and to inspire your curiosity and creativity so you'll see new solutions to *your* problems.

This chapter will focus on using generative AI to generate original text-based content of one kind or another. The next chapter will do the same but for non-text content like images, audio, and videos.

Automating accuracy checking

If you haven't yet noticed, we'll be focusing mostly on OpenAI tools like GPT in this book. That's not to say there aren't other powerful and effective resources out there for getting this stuff done. There are. But right now at least, OpenAI has the most creativity and momentum in the industry, and it's where most of the groundbreaking action is happening.

To be honest, I can already see subtle indications that this might be starting to change. I wouldn't be surprised if 12 months from now Google or even an independent platform was leading the way forward. But you use the tools you've got. And right now, most of those tools are, one way or another, connected to OpenAI.

So GPT it will be. The thing about GPT Playground (https://platform.openai.com/playground) is that it's supposed to make you think about *program code* rather than *chat sessions*. In other words, how can the Playground's View Code feature help you build an automated workflow?

Let's imagine that you're trying to integrate GPT creation into a larger process. Perhaps your organization is encouraging its website users to post their own thoughts and comments on your public discussion forum.

Since the product or service you provide is technically complex, you have an interest in maintaining a high level of dialogue on the platform. On the other hand, you don't have the time and resources to manually edit each and every user comment before it goes public. Instead, you decide you'd rather have GPT do the work for you. Figure 3.1 shows how that would look in Playground.

Figure 3.1   GPT Playground using the Edit mode

Note how the Mode drop-down is set to the value of `Chat`. This gives me a `SYSTEM` field in addition to the `USER` and `Output` fields to the Playground interface. Here, I entered some text containing an obvious error into the Input field:

DA The most famous musicians from the 1960s were the Beatles, Bob Dylan, and J. S. Bach

I then typed `Check for accuracy and and output a corrected version` as my instruction. When I submitted the prompt, the output came back with "Elvis Presley" as the third item in the list. Here it is as code:

```python
from openai import OpenAI
client = OpenAI()

response = client.chat.completions.create(
  model="gpt-4",
  messages=[
    {
      "role": "system",
      "content": "Check for accuracy and output a corrected version"
    },
    {
      "role": "user",
      "content": "The most famous musicians from the 1960's were the
 Beatles, Bob Dylan, and J.S. Bach"
    }
  ],
  temperature=1,
  max_tokens=256,
  top_p=1,
  frequency_penalty=0,
  presence_penalty=0
)
```

When I ran that code through the API, I got a slightly different response:

```
response
<OpenAIObject chat.completion id=chatcmpl-7l0C8xGXBTM9quFZoPwDHHaSl
7avX at 0x7f07e67109a0> JSON: {
  "choices": [
    {
      "finish_reason": "stop",
      "index": 0,
      "message": {
        "content": "The most famous musicians from the 1960's were
        the Beatles, Bob Dylan, and Jimi Hendrix.",
        "role": "assistant"
      }
    }
  ],
  "created": 1691436520,
  "id": "chatcmpl-7l0C8xGXBTM9quFZoPwDHHaSl7avX",
  "model": "gpt-4-0613",
  "object": "chat.completion",
  "usage": {
    "completion_tokens": 23,
    "prompt_tokens": 41,
    "total_tokens": 64
  }
}
```

Figure 3.2 shows how I can also filter content for our use-case example based on keywords using the `Stop sequences` field. This can be helpful if I'd like to catch and prevent the use of inappropriate words in user posts altogether. I'm sure you could come up with your own list of even less appropriate words that could be added to this field.

Figure 3.2   GPT Playground using the Edit mode with `Stop sequences`

Naturally, you'll need to make your own decision whether it's appropriate to give GPT the power to effectively censor your users. While I would be nervous giving AI that kind of authority, that example is really about illustrating possibilities.

Use the OpenAI Playground (or other resources) to build workflows that use large language model (LLM) functionality to parse text in real time and check for accuracy.

Creating new contextually aware content

This section is going to be fun—unless you're not into fun, of course. Don't let me get in your way. By all means, feel free to skip ahead.

But the rest of us are going to dive deep into the strange world of generating fiction on-demand, which is not to say that I would ever advise you to try to earn money selling AI-generated fiction. It's hard enough getting genuine human-sourced fiction noticed amongst the millions of titles competing for readers' attention on Amazon. Instead, the fiction angle is really only here as another way to get you thinking creatively. As it turns out, I don't even read fiction.

So where could such creativity lead you? Well, consider how much time and effort you could save configuring an AI model to generate annual company reports. The AI would need to be familiar with your company's operations (i.e., be contextually aware). So it would need to

- Ingest your company's complex financial history
- Ingest the details of its most recent fiscal year
- Understand the reporting requirements of your industry and local regulators

With all that taken care of, you'll be just a mouse click away from automated business documents. But that would be a bit complicated to simulate. So instead, I'll use this fan-fiction example to illustrate the process.

My plan, as illustrated in figure 3.3, is to have GPT index a large collection of existing novels written by a single author that features a largely fixed cast of core characters. Once the index exists, I'll try to confirm that GPT is familiar with all the events of the complete set of novels and then get it to write new content using the original style and characters. Hopefully, the new works will also be internally consistent and free of historical contradictions.

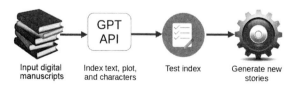

Figure 3.3. The workflow necessary for indexing and processing a single author's public domain books and generating new stories

Anyway, to get my plan going, I first asked ChatGPT the following question:

 Is there a series of famous English-language novels that are now all in the public domain that follow the same set of characters through multiple books?

True to form, ChatGPT came through, reminding me of the Sherlock Holmes series by Sir Arthur Conan Doyle, the Tarzan series by Edgar Rice Burroughs, the Anne of Green Gables series by Lucy Maud Montgomery, and the Tom Swift Series by Victor Appleton. Excellent. I'll go with Sherlock.

I'll browse over to the Project Gutenberg site (https://www .gutenberg.org/), where 70,000 public domain e-books live, just waiting for you to come by and enjoy them. Most of the books are older classics whose copyrights have expired according to at least US copyright laws. As you can see from the image, books are available in a wide range of formats (figure 3.4).

Figure 3.4.   The many formats available on a Shakespeare collection page on the Project Gutenberg site

I'll then download the plain text versions covering around 25 novels and short stories from the original Sherlock Holmes series. I'll save those files to the `data/` directory beneath the location where my Python code will run.

Setting up your environment for Python

For this exercise, I'll assume you've got the Python programming language installed along with the Python package manager, `pip`. For help with getting Python itself set up for your operating system, see the official download page (https://www.python.org/downloads/). For everything you need to know about `pip`, see https://pip.pypa.io/en/stable/installation/. Or just head over to the appendix A for instructions for installing Python.

> **NOTE** Anaconda or `venv` are alternatives to `pip`.

If you don't yet have a valid OpenAI API key, you can get one by signing up on the OpenAI API reference page (https://platform .openai.com/docs/api-reference).

From here on in, you'll need to work within a Python environment. One way to make that happen is by typing `python` from a command line. Everything you type into such an environment will be handled by the Python interpreter. You could also create a plain text file and, when you've added all the code you'll need, run it from the command line using something like this:

```
python myfilename.py
```

On some systems, you'll need to make that `python3` rather than `python`.

My personal favorite Python environment, though, is JupyterLab (https://jupyter.org/). Jupyter will give you a browser-based environment that comes with all kinds of optimizations for managing serious data workloads. Another environment that's particularly popular for Python work is Google's Colab (https://colab.google/).

Creating your prompt (using Python)

Here's how you'll import all the necessary Python modules that'll actually run our code:

```
from llama_index import SimpleDirectoryReader
from llama_index.node_parser import SimpleNodeParser
from llama_index import GPTVectorStoreIndex
import os
```

By the way, this will cost you some money in API charges. When I ran it myself, it probably set me back around $0.25.

If you haven't net installed a module on your system, running something like this will get you there:

```
pip install llama_index
```

Next, you'll create an environment variable to hold your OpenAI API key. Make sure you replace sk-xxxx with your actual key:

```
os.environ['OPENAI_API_KEY'] = "sk-xxxx"
```

This will load the contents of any documents in the data/ directory and read them to the variable documents:

```
documents = SimpleDirectoryReader('data').load_data()
```

The next three lines use the parser.get_nodes_from_documents method to convert the actual contents of our data/ directory to a GPT-friendly index. Depending on how much data you've got, this step could take a while:

```
parser = SimpleNodeParser()
nodes = parser.get_nodes_from_documents(documents)
index = GPTVectorStoreIndex(nodes)
```

Finally, we'll pass our prompt and run it against the index:

```
response = index.query("Taking into account the plot and character \
    details of all of the stories in these documents, are there \
    any contradictions between events in any one story \
        and events in any other?")
print(response)
```

I began with this question about contradictions between books for two reasons:

- Because this is a reasonably reliable way to confirm that the model has actually read and understood the content

- Because I'm actually curious to see whether Doyle himself had trouble keeping all his details straight

Here's the response I got when I submitted that prompt:

 No, there are no contradictions between events in any one story and events in any other. All of the stories in these documents are connected by the same characters and plot points, and the events in each story are consistent with the events in the other stories, including the new context provided. The fragment of paper found between the finger and thumb of the dead man is consistent with the events in the other stories, as it appears to be an appointment and the hour mentioned upon it is the very time at which the poor fellow met his fate.

That's good enough for this experiment, but it definitely wouldn't do for projects where accuracy is critical. After all, when I asked the regular ChatGPT the same question, I was given no less than five factual discrepancies. Of those, however, Watson's war wound being somehow in both his arm ("A Study in Scarlet") and leg ("The Sign of Four") was the only one that truly met my criteria. The bottom line: independently confirm any AI output on which you plan to rely for important operations.

Here's my prompt asking for the opening paragraphs of a brand-new Sherlock Holmes story:

```
response = index.query("Write the first two paragraphs of a new \
    story using the same characters, ambience, and writing \
    style as the documents in data/ The story should follow a \
    plot involving the theft of an entire passenger liner in the \
    Cunard line.")
print(response)
```

Here's what came back:

 I had heard the rumors of a daring heist, but I never expected it to be true. A passenger liner in the Cunard line had been stolen in its entirety, and the authorities were at a loss as to how it had been done. I had to find out the truth, and so I made my way to the docks, where I knew I would find the answers I sought.

As I waited, I passed down the steps, worn hollow in the centre by the ceaseless tread of drunken feet. By the light of a flickering oil-lamp above the door, I found the latch and made my way into a long, low

(continued)

room, thick and heavy with the brown opium smoke, and terraced with wooden berths, like the forecastle of an emigrant ship. Through the gloom, I could dimly make out the figures of men lying in strange, fantastic poses, bowed shoulders, bent knees, heads thrown back, and chins pointing upward. Out of the black shadows, there glimmered little red circles of light, now bright, now faint, as the burning poison waxed or waned in the bowls of the metal pipes.

Suddenly, I heard a commotion from the street outside. I rushed

Sounds dark. But it's actually darker than you think: when I did a bit of poking around, I found that GPT had stolen that second paragraph more or less intact from one of the existing stories that was included in the documents: "The Man with the Twisted Lip."

So I asked again, this time adding `but without using any verbatim quotations`. The new results were more original and, I guess, more or less credible.

Copyright restrictions

Now is probably a good time to talk about copyright restrictions. As you saw, the original Sherlock Holmes stories are all in the public domain, so there's no problem reusing their content, characters, or plot lines. Generating content based on protected works—much like works of fan fiction—is more complicated. In many jurisdictions, there may be allowances for content that can be classified as fair use, transformative work, or noncommercial work. Just make sure you do your research in advance.

As mentioned in chapter 1, it's also possible that any content you use to feed an AI model will be archived and even used by the organization provider (like OpenAI). This could be a problem for owners of copyrighted creative or sensitive business data.

The point is that AI can "understand" and index the contents of enormous data archives and use those as a resource for building new content—like annual financial reports.

Generating specialized documents

There's a certain unmatchable advantage to having an instant recall-level knowledge of the entire internet, even if it's only the pre-2022 version. Troubleshooting even deeply uncommon technical or household problems is now easy. There's no detail too obscure or abstract, no process too involved, and no product assembly guide too obscure. Forever gone is the correlation between marital friction and putting Ikea furniture together.

That's great if your name, dear reader, happens to be GPT. (And why shouldn't it be? What's to stop me from creating a GPT agent that runs around the internet buying all the available copies of my book and then happily reading them over and over again?) The rest of us, however, will have to satisfy our technical needs through the medium of AI prompts.

But getting the most out of AI does require that we have at least some domain knowledge of our own. Contract law, a field that requires gallons of domain knowledge, is one area where GPT can shine. After all, GPT-4 has already passed the Uniform Bar Exam, scoring in the 90th percentile.

A great deal of what lawyers do when preparing new contracts involves manipulating templated blocks of text. They'll generally have two goals:

- To accurately identify the assets and principals involved
- To protect their clients from potential loss of rights

Well, manipulating templated blocks of text while closely complying with a clearly stated set of facts and anticipating well-documented possible perils is a perfect use case for a mature, well-trained LLM. To demonstrate that, I prompted ChatGPT with the following request:

 Draft a contract for me that formalizes the relationship between David Clinton of 123 Any St., Smallville, Ohio, USA with Manning Publishers in which David Clinton will provide ongoing consulting services to Manning in exchange for a 75% share in all net revenues.

The response was remarkable (although I have no idea why it arbitrarily dropped my share of Manning's profits from 75% to 15%). There's no reason to reproduce the contract here, but you (along with any interested Manning executives) are free to view it on my website (https://bootstrap-it.com/contract_sample.pdf). I'm no lawyer, but I've signed more than a few contracts through my career, and this draft really seemed to cover all the key elements.

> **NOTE** Once again, however, I must emphasize that AI is still nothing more than a dumb computer that doesn't really know what it's doing. Never automatically rely on anything that comes from an LLM. And, as GPT itself warned me when delivering that contract, it would be wise to seek a professional opinion before executing it.

Here's where domain knowledge (the specialized understanding and expertise one has for a particular subject) comes in. No matter how impressive your LLM's results may be, without your own general understanding of a field, the risk of misunderstanding, misinterpreting, and misapplying the generated content is high. How else can you be sure your output isn't missing important context or making outright errors?

And even if you are an experienced specialist within a particular domain, it'll be hard to be sure the thousands of words your AI gives you don't contain a few broken details or confusing language. For many applications, "mostly accurate" is just not good enough.

Here's where the kind of *specialized* AI projects I'm seeing more frequently can help. For example, take the website Harvey.ai (https://www.harvey.ai/blog). The people behind the site appear to be using their legal and technological expertise to offer law firms access to a specialized AI. But what they're offering goes far beyond the silly contract I discussed a moment ago. Harvey is clearly using the considerable expertise—meaning, domain knowledge—of its creators to make their service more accurate, predictable, and useful.

No matter how much law-related information general tools like GPT might have ingested, they'll never be able to compete with a specialized AI. There's room for domain experts to add significant value to the service.

This can apply far beyond just law. Whatever it is that you do well can probably be used for a productive partnership with AI to provide customer-facing services. Here are some particularly useful categories of content where LLMs combined with human domain expertise can be effective:

- Insights, explanations, and tutorials on a wide range of technology topics, such as programming languages, artificial intelligence, cybersecurity, blockchain, and emerging technologies.
- Scientific content produced as explainers, research summaries, and detailed articles on subjects like physics, chemistry, biology, astronomy, and environmental science.
- Healthcare content like patient education materials, information on diseases, medical procedures, and research developments, along with insights into emerging healthcare technologies.
- Finance and economics content can include real-time market analysis, investment insights, economic forecasts, financial concept explainers, and customizable guidance on personal finance, budgeting, and retirement planning.
- Marketing and advertising content can include generating marketing strategies, ad content, social media posts, product descriptions, and consumer behavior and trend analytics.
- Education materials can include lesson plans, explanations of academic concepts, and assistance in various subjects such as mathematics, history, literature, and foreign languages.
- AI platforms can provide travel guides, recommendations for tourist destinations, tips for planning trips, and insights into local culture and customs.

Use large volumes of existing data to train your LLM to generate content that's both aware of existing constraints and capable of adopting a specific writing voice and style. And be aware that training should incorporate domain-specific knowledge and constraints.

Generating programming code

Domain knowledge is also helpful when looking for assistance with your programming code. Asking GPT for help will be far more effective if you already have a fairly clear understanding of what the code you're after is meant to accomplish. But it's also important to have a general familiarity with common coding structures and design, like loops, variables, and conditional statements.

That means a prompt like

> **DA** Show me how to build a website.

won't be nearly as effective as

> **DA** Show me how to build a responsive, full-stack web page that incorporates HTML, CSS, JavaScript, Node.js, and SQLite.

You should also never assume that the code your AI gives you will actually work. When something does fail to run, be sure to note the precise error messages you see. Then you can go back and use those as you ask for more help.

Interactive coding with Copilot

An interactive chat coding session with an AI can feel an awful lot like pair programming. And that's a good thing. In fact, the name they chose for what is probably the most popular GPT-based code support tools around now is GitHub's Copilot (https://docs.github .com/en/copilot), which says it all.

I won't go too deeply into the general topic because it's been well documented online and, even better, because Nathan B. Crocker has focused on it in *AI-Powered Developer: Build Great Software with ChatGPT and Copilot* (Manning, 2024; https://www.manning.com/ books/ai-powered-developer). But I will quickly take you through the process of getting up to speed with Copilot. The first thing to know is that after your 30-day free trial, Copilot charges a monthly fee.

There are two ways to use Copilot: GitHub Copilot for Individuals is available for personal GitHub accounts, and GitHub Copilot for Business can be used by organizations. Verified students, teachers, and maintainers of popular open source projects can be eligible for free access.

Once you enable Copilot within your GitHub account and then set up your payment preferences, you'll need to choose a code editor. At this point, Copilot is compatible with Visual Studio, Visual Studio Code, Neovim, and JetBrains IDEs. Whichever IDE you choose, you'll need to find and install the GitHub Copilot extension.

Once you've got everything enabled and installed and you're logged into your GitHub account, you can start using Copilot. As you write code in your preferred programming language, Copilot will provide code suggestions in real time based on the context and patterns it's learned from its training data. You can accept the suggestions by pressing Tab, and Copilot will generate code snippets to speed up your development process.

Copilot understands code structure and descriptive naming usage. Using an example from the Copilot documentation, you could begin with nothing more than a JavaScript (`.js`) file containing a single function header like this:

```
function calculateDaysBetweenDates(begin, end) {
```

Copilot can take that and build a complete working function that might work right out of the box.

Try this for yourself

Use `llama_index`—the way you saw with the stories of Sherlock Holmes—on as much of your writing as you can to train GPT to speak for you. Then prompt your model to respond to specific questions or scenarios using your style.

Can we handle all that new content?

Summary

- Use the GPT Playground to learn how to apply AI models, completion configurations, and environmental controls to your prompts. The Playground is also an excellent source of code for API-directed prompts and automation.
- Train your AI model using existing data/content and incorporating domain-specific constraints to create optimally suitable new content.
- Generative AI tools have been widely adopted for help with programming code, but purpose-built tools like GitHub's Copilot can be particularly effective, given how they've been trained on the entire GitHub site. Use code-assistant tools to build on your existing programming ideas and code.

Creating with media resources

Text and programming code are natural targets for generative AI. After all, after binary, those are the languages with which your computer has the most experience. So, intuitively, the ability to generate the kinds of resources we discussed in the previous chapter was expected.

But images, audio, and video would be a very different story. That's because visual and audio data

- Are inherently more complex and high-dimensional than text
- Lack symbolic representations and have more nuanced meaning, making it challenging to directly apply traditional programming techniques
- Can be highly subjective and ambiguous, making it difficult to build automated systems that can consistently and accurately interpret such data
- Lack inherent context, making it harder for computer systems to confidently derive meaning
- Require significant computational resources for processing

Nevertheless, tools for generating media resources have been primary drivers of the recent explosion of interest in AI. So the rest of this chapter will be dedicated to exploring the practical use of AI-driven digital media creation services.

Generating images

First off, just how does a large language model (LLM) convert a text prompt into a visual artifact? Figure 4.1 illustrates the key steps making up the training process that makes this happen.

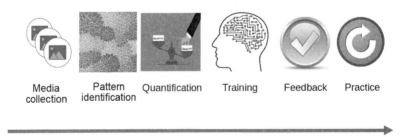

Media   Pattern   Quantification   Training   Feedback   Practice
collection   identification

Figure 4.1.   The training process for building a media-generation LLM

Here are the steps of that process in more detail:

1 Gather a huge collection of audio, images, and videos to learn from. These examples come from all over the internet and cover a wide range of styles and topics.

2 Use the examples to learn patterns. For audio, it learns the different sounds and how they relate to each other (like how a melody follows a certain rhythm). For images, it learns what different objects look like and how they appear together. For videos, it figures out how different shots are put together to tell a story.

3 Apply mathematical magic to convert the audio, images, and videos into representative numbers. These numbers help the system understand the patterns and relationships in the content. It's like the system is translating the art into a language it can understand.

4 Train the model involves having the LLM search for the best patterns that can recreate the audio, images, and videos it's seen.

5 When the LLM creates something, we apply feedback and adjustments by comparing it to real examples. The model adjusts its patterns to get better at creating content that's closer to what we want.

6 The LLM practices (a lot) by creating new audio, images, and videos. With each practice round, it gets better and better at understanding the patterns and making its own content.

It's important to note that AI-generated images and videos are nothing more than dumb computers' best efforts based on learned patterns from the training data and may not always reflect real-world accuracy—which should be obvious for those of us who have seen AI-generated humans with 6 to 10 fingers per hand, really weird teeth, or three arms. For context, two is traditionally the maximum number of arms attached to any one human at a given time. And, no, I have no clue why LLMs get this obvious thing so wrong, so often.

Providing detailed prompts

Whichever image-generation service you use, the way you build your prompts will go a long way to determining the quality of the images that come out the other end. You'll want to be descriptive while also defining the style of the image you want. Therefore, a prompt like "some trees" won't be nearly as effective as "a sunlit wooded area in the style of John Constable." That latter example contains a *subject* ("wooded area"), *adjective* ("sunlit"), and an *artistic style* ("John Constable"). You should try to include at least one of each of those three elements in your prompts. Feel free to add details like colors and background textures. In case you're curious, figure 4.2 shows what the Stable Diffusion model gave me in response to that last prompt.

Figure 4.2.   A Stable Diffusion image in the style of English Romantic painter John Constable

When it comes to styles, consider adding something from this (partial) list:

- Photograph
- Cubist

- Oil painting
- Matte
- Surreal
- Steampunk
- Cute creatures
- Fantasy worlds
- Cyberpunk
- Old
- Renaissance painting
- Abstract
- Realistic
- Expressionism
- Comic
- Ink

Prompting for images

Nonetheless, I decided to ignore all that advice about styles and details and ask a few AI image creation platforms for possible covers to adorn this book. My prompt, as you can see, didn't provide any specific descriptions. Instead, I gave it nothing more than an abstraction (the book title) and assumed the generative AI tool would be able to translate the concept hinted at into something graphic:

 Create a 6:9 cover for a book entitled "The Complete Obsolete Guide to Generative AI." The image should contain no text or alphanumeric characters.

It is useful to note how I specified the aspect ratio (6:9) to tell the software what shape the image should take. I also told it not to include any text. AI is notoriously *awful* at text.

In case anyone in the Manning art department is reading, here are a couple of the images I got back. The first image, shown in figure 4.3, came from DreamStudio and looks great, although they did seem to miss the memo on aspect ratio.

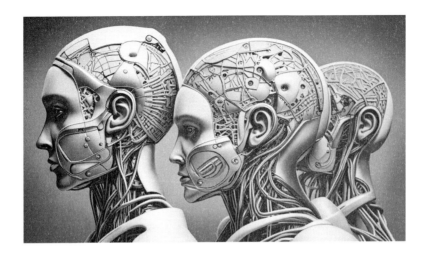

Figure 4.3.   **A DreamStudio book cover image**

The image from the Stable Diffusion model, shown in figure 4.4, hits a lot of the right marks and, considering how little I gave it to work with, is pretty impressive.

Figure 4.4. A Stable Diffusion book cover image

I find more image-generation services every time I look online. But, right now, the particularly big players are Midjourney, DALL-E, Stable Diffusion, and Dream Studio,

Midjourney is a bit tricky to get started but seems to produce a very high quality of images. You'll need to create an account at https://www.midjourney.com/, select a yearly or monthly fee account level, and then add a Midjourney server to your Discord account. From Discord, you can select the Midjourney Bot that should appear within the Direct Messages column in Discord (figure 4.5). To get your first set of images, enter your prompt after typing /imagine in the text field at the bottom. Four possible images, once they're generated, will appear in your Midjourney UI. I can't say I understand why it's designed that way, but a lot of people seem to feel it's worth the effort.

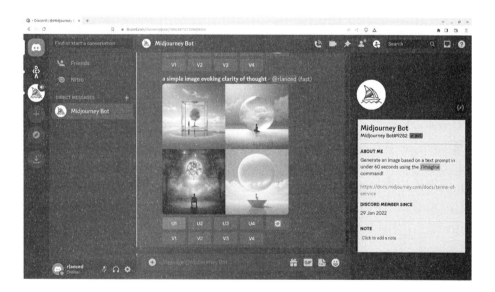

Figure 4.5.   Midjourney accessed within a Discord account

DALL-E—a product of OpenAI—was the first digital image-generating tool most of us encountered (figure 4.6). In its time, it was shocking and brought a lot of attention to the underlying technologies and related possibilities. DALL-E is available from the regular ChatGPT prompt interface for accounts with a Plus subscription

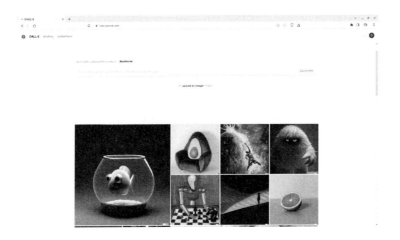

Figure 4.6.   OpenAI's DALL-E browser-based interface

Stable Diffusion is a freely available generative model that can be accessed through an account with services like Hugging Face (https://huggingface.co/)—a hosting service for many AI models, datasets, and other AI tools using both free and pay-as-you-go levels. If you have a computer with a graphic processor unit (GPU) and at least 8 GB of video memory, you can install and run your own private Stable Diffusion service (https://stable-diffusion-ui.github.io/; figure 4.7).

**Figure 4.7.
The Stable
Diffusion
GitHub page**

DreamStudio offers image generation through its website (https://beta.dreamstudio.ai/generate; see figure 4.8). You're permitted a limited number of credits for free, with more available for purchase. Currently, usage costs $10 for every 1,000 credits. Costs per image depend on size and complexity. DreamStudio is provided by stability.ai, the company responsible for Stable Diffusion.

Figure 4.8.   The DreamStudio browser interface

In addition, a Plus subscription with ChatGPT will expand the capabilities of the regular chat tool to include image generation. In fact, at the time of writing, Plus gives you built-in access to DALL-E version 3.

Generating video

If generative AIs can create images, couldn't they do the same trick with video too? Well, of course they can. But you will have to be a bit more specific about what you mean by *video*.

If what you're looking for is the ability to write a prompt (like the ones we've been using for images) and a beautiful video suddenly springs to life, well, we're not quite there yet. Meta and Google have both loudly announced technologies (Make-a-Video for Meta and Imagen Video for Google) that'll do just that. But bear in mind that both those tools will absolutely, certainly, and without a doubt be available on some unspecified date in the future.

RunwayML did release a promising tool with limited access. But, considering the current 4- to 15-second maximums per output clip and the significant rendering times, it's not exactly everything we're hoping for yet.

However, if you can expand your definition of *video* a little bit wider, then we might have something to talk about.

AI-assisted video editing

One process that most certainly does exist right now involves taking existing videos and manipulating them so they tell a very different story. Using stylization and masking effects, applications like RunwayML's Gen-1 (https://runwayml.com/)and the open source project Tex2Live (https://github.com/omerbt/Text2LIVE) can create things that high-end Hollywood studios have been doing for a while. The difference is that those Hollywood studios often spent many months and millions of dollars for the equipment and experts they needed. We can now get pretty much the same quality in a few seconds on a modestly powered laptop. In fact, you can self-host Text2Live by downloading it and running it on your own machine.

What can you actually do? I'd recommend you check out both the Gen-1 and Text2Live sites for demo videos. They'll show you how textures, backgrounds, lighting, and other attributes can be swapped in and out to convert an existing video of, say, a man running down a driveway into an astronaut running across an alien planet's surface.

Text-to-video slide shows

That's all great fun. But some of us use video for tasks that live closer to the office than outer space. In other words, there's a huge market for media content focused on education, IT training, news services, marketing, and corporate communications. Putting together such presentations the traditional way can take hours for each minute of video (I know because I do that for a living). And that's not taking into account the extra equipment and studio costs it'll take to put you directly on camera.

There are, however, AI-driven services that can take your script and generate a professional video consisting of a hyperrealistic computer-generated voice (using your choice of male or female, accent, age, and personality) and appropriate supporting background images and bullet-point text. You can upload your own images too. The high-end players in this genre will add a human-like avatar who looks pretty close to an actual live human being. Add in a script generated using ChatGPT the way we've seen in previous chapters, and you'll be going from zero to a complete set of professional videos in minutes.

What's the catch? Ah, yes. The catch. Well, the high-end stuff isn't cheap. Many of the more professional services currently charge hundreds of dollars a year (or more) and limit output to a specified number of minutes of video each month. Arguably, the leaders in this market include

- Synthesia (https://www.synthesia.io/)
- Elai (https://app.elai.io/)
- Steve AI (https://www.steve.ai/)
- Fliki (https://fliki.ai/)
- Synthesys (not to be confused with Synthesia (https://synthesys.io/)

Generating presentation resources

There's something about PowerPoint presentations that inspires both fear and loathing. There's the loathing from meeting participants who are condemned to suffer through poorly planned and designed presentations. And then there's the dread experienced by presenters as they face the unwanted task of painstakingly building their presentations slide by slide (and then suffering the hatred of the victims in their audiences).

And, of course, slide decks are about far more than just conference presentations. They're often also the backbone structure of business and educational videos, which is where this chapter's topic comes in.

You see, generative AI is already perfectly capable of doing all the hard work for you: sometimes technological innovations actually do solve problems. At least as far as presenters or video creators go, their poor audiences are still pretty much on their own.

Gamma (https://gamma.app/) is an example of one of many text-to-presentation-deck services out there. I'll focus on Gamma for this illustration simply because that's the one with which I've had the most experience so far.

Working with some of the free introductory credits I'm allowed, I selected the `New with AI` option, followed by the `Text transform` path, and entered this text in the instructions field (yup, that's this chapter's working title):

> **DA** Generate a presentation on the topic of Creating with Generative AI: Media Resources using these headings:
> - Generating images
> - Generating video
> - AI-assisted video editing
> - Text to video slide shows
> - Generating presentation resources
> - Generating music

After that, I only had to choose a format from the list, and within a couple of minutes, Gamma had generated the text content, layout, and visuals for a really attractive presentation. You can see the PDF that was generated on my website (https://bootstrap-it.com/GammaDeck.pdf).

Naturally, I'm free to edit any content that doesn't fit my needs. But this is a game changer for those of us longing to escape PowerPoint prison.

Generating voice

Not happy with your accent or just don't have a nice, quiet place to record your podcast or video narration? There are services that'll take text content and generate audio files with your choice of voice, accent, perfect pacing, and no kids screaming in the background. If you'd prefer to be the narrator after all, you can also have your voice cloned so it can be used to generate your audio files.

Of course, voice-to-text has been happening for decades. We've all heard voicemail systems featuring computer-generated voices. What's changing is that advances in AI have greatly improved the quality.

Improved doesn't necessarily mean perfected. Try it yourself. Upload some content to, say, Amazon's Polly service (https://aws .amazon.com/polly/), and you'll be impressed. But after listening carefully for at least a minute, any listener will probably conclude that this isn't really a human being speaking, and as good as it is, it's quality will never be confused for Orson Welles or Winston Churchill. On the other hand, hiring a human being with that level of oratorical skills to record your content would cost you considerably more than the $4.00 for every *million* characters Amazon will charge you. So there's that.

Polly is primarily aimed at organizations that need to generate voice in real time. Think interactive website support systems or content accessibility. That means Polly's customers are going to want programmatic API connections to script the creation and management of their audio. To show you how that'll work, here's a sample command using the AWS CLI (a command-line API access tool) that will request an audio .MP3 file generated from the text in a local file I called text.txt. To make this work, you'll need an AWS account. You'll also need to have the AWS CLI set up and configured (https:// mng.bz/Ado7):

```
aws polly start-speech-synthesis-task \
    --output-s3-bucket-name mypolly345 \
    --text file://text.txt \
    --voice-id Matthew \
```

```
--engine neural \
--language-code en-US \
--output-format mp3
```

Note how I specified the `Matthew` voice using a US English (`en-US`) accent. Polly has dozens of other voices and accent options.

I can download the file from the specified Amazon S3 output bucket once it's generated with this AWS CLI command:

```
# Copy all files:
aws s3 cp s3://mypolly345 . --recursive
```

And I can remove remote copies of those files using `s3 rm` with

```
# Remove all existing files:
aws s3 rm s3://mypolly345/ --recursive
```

because I believe you should always clean up your toys when you're finished playing with them.

Text-to-speech is a crowded market. Besides Polly, other platforms offer API-accessed services. Those would include Google Cloud's cleverly named Text-to-Speech (https://cloud.google.com/text-to-speech/) and IBM's Watson Text to Speech Voices (https://www.ibm.com/products/text-to-speech).

Besides those, there are also services that'll let you convert text documents to speech one at a time through a website interface. ElevenLabs (https://beta.elevenlabs.io/) has a reputation as an over-performer in this field, particularly when it comes to creating custom voices or cloning your voice. Speechify (https://speechify.com/) is another big player.

Audio transcriptions

That takes care of text-to-audio. But what about audio-to-text (otherwise known as *speech recognition*)? There's no shortage of business uses for transcribing existing video or audio files. Can't think of any offhand? Well, how about taking the audio from a (boring) 2-hour video conference that you missed? Even though your boss bought your my-dog-ate-my-homework excuse at the time, you still have to get back up to speed by watching the recording of the conference.

You didn't get to where you are now without being good and lazy. So here's how you're going to push back against that evil decree.

You'll submit the recording to an audio transcription service, which will deliver you a text document containing a full script. You'll then convert the script to a PDF file and upload it to the ChatPDF service we'll discuss in chapter 5. When the PDF is uploaded, you can request a brief but accurate summary of the script.

One example of a service that offers simple but effective summaries is Summarize.tech (https://www.summarize.tech/). To test it out, I fed the address of one of my own YouTube videos (https://www.youtube.com/@davidbclinton) into its URL field. Within a few short seconds, I was looking at this brief but accurate summary:

> *This video discusses the security vulnerabilities that are associated with AWS EC2 instances. By default, these instances lack a firewall and have an open security group, making them vulnerable to attack. The instructor provides a real-life example of launching an EC2 instance with open incoming traffic and receiving login attempts within minutes. He stresses the importance of striking a balance between server functionality and infrastructure security, which will be the main goal of the course.*

See? Life isn't half as horrible as it looked when you rolled out of bed this morning.

Naturally, there are also APIs for transcribing audio. Two are OpenAI's Whisper (https://github.com/openai/whisper) and Google's Speech-to-Text (https://cloud.google.com/speech-to-text).

Whisper is a dog that does lots of tricks. Among other things, it can handle language identification, speech translation, and multilingual speech recognition. Like many GPT-based apps, Whisper is built to be installed and run on your own computer using a valid OpenAI API key, which, as you've already seen can be acquired on the OpenAI site (https://platform.openai.com/account/api-keys).

And that's not going to be half as complicated as you think. Within a Python environment, just use `pip` to install the Whisper package:

```
pip install -U openai-whisper
```

You'll also need the open source video/audio management tool, ffmpeg. Here's how installing that into a Debian/Ubuntu-based Linux system will work:

```
sudo apt update && sudo apt install ffmpeg
```

And here's the code that'll make it work:

```
import whisper

model = whisper.load_model("base")
result = model.transcribe("MyAudio.flac")
print(result["text"])
```

We'll use the `base` model, write our transcribed text (based on the `MyAudio.flac` input file I was using) to the variable `result` and then display the result. Super simple. And it's surprisingly accurate!

Of course, you can use all the regular audio and video file formats as inputs and select from one of five models (tiny, base, small, medium, and large).

Generating music

I guess I can't move on without talking about AI-generated music. I'm not just talking about ChatGPT-powered lyrics or even software that outputs sheet music, but *actual* music. That means software that lets you specify details like genre, the instruments you want playing, the emotional tone, tempo range, time signature, key signature, and harmonic repetition, and real music comes out the other end.

As you've probably heard, some of those services also make it possible to recreate near-perfect sound-alikes of famous singers and have them sing your own new music. The exact legal implications of the use of such sound-alikes are not yet clear.

Online AI music generation tools—most of which are primarily designed for creating background music using various genres—include AIVA (https://www.aiva.ai/), boomy (https://boomy .com/), Soundful (https://soundful.com/), and Mubert (https:// mubert.com/). More recently, Meta (the owner of Facebook) released two audio generation tools as open source (https://github .com/facebookresearch/audiocraft):

- MusicGen will generate music from text prompts.
- AudioGen will give you sound effects (think "busy street with police car siren" or "wind blowing through trees").

In addition, Meta also released the neural audio codec, EnCodec, and the diffusion-based decoder, Multi Band Diffusion. You can freely download the code, but just like working with image generators, you will need substantial system resources to make it work.

Try this for yourself

Why not produce an original training video using some of the media generation tools we've seen in this chapter? Here's how you might want to go about it:

- Pick a topic ("How to make the most out of generative AI tools," perhaps) and prompt an LLM for a video transcript (a 3-minute video will require around 500 words of text).
- Ask the LLM to summarize the script to give you a set of descriptive bullet points.
- Using Gamma (https://gamma.app/), select Create New > Text Transform and paste your bullet points into the content field. Then, generate slides.
- Using Amazon Polly, generate a narration file out of the script created by your LLM.
- Use Mubert to generate background music.
- Assemble your narration, slides, and background music into a video using, say, the Vimeo video maker (https://vimeo.com/create/customize?hash=storyboard_601142419_1000).
- Finally, just for fun, use Whisper to extract a text transcript from the narration track on your video and see how close it is to the original script.

TIP Don't forget to check in once in a while for updates to the Generative AI Resources list https://github.com/dbclinton/Complete_Obsolete_Guide_AI/blob/main/GenAI_Resources .md in the book's GitHub repo.

If AI generated it and AI consumed it, did it actually happen?

Summary

- We learned about generating digital images (and video) using services like Stable Diffusion and MidJourney.
- We learned about tools that can use AI to transform existing video artifacts into new media,
- We learned how to use AI tools like Gamma to generate presentation slide stacks from text prompts,
- We learned about audio-to-text and text-to-audio transcribing using tools like Amazon Polly and OpenAI Whisper.

5

Feeding data to your generative AI models

This chapter covers

- Building and then querying an index based on a local data archive
- Uploading a PDF document to the ChatPDF service to query it the way you'd use ChatGPT
- Scripting the PDF-querying process using the ChatPDF API
- Using the AutoGPT tool to give a GPT-fueled agent access to the full and open internet

There's only so long you'll keep at it before the novelty of torturing secrets out of an always friendly (and occasionally outrageous) AI gets a bit stale. After all, how many versions of the perfect résumé do you need? And do you really want to hear how John Lennon would have sounded singing Shakespearean sonnets?

The real power of a large language model (LLM) is in how quickly it's able to process and "understand" insane volumes of data. It would be a shame to limit its scope to just the stuff it was shown during its training period. And in any case, you stand to gain more from how your AI processes your data than someone else's. Just imagine how much value can be unleashed by identifying:

- Patterns and trends in health records
- Threats and attacks in digital network access logs
- Potential financial opportunities or risks in banking records
- Opportunities for introducing efficiencies in supply chain, infrastructure, and governance operations
- Insurance, tax, or program fraud
- Government corruption (and opportunities for operational improvements)

So, is it possible to expose GPT to stuff on your computer or, even better, to stuff that's out there on the live internet? The short answer is yes. And that'll have to do for the long answer, too. In fact, as of a few hours before I sat down to write this chapter, there are a handful of ways to get this done. In this chapter, I'll show you how to send LLMs deep into your data-rich documents and out across the live internet.

Indexing local data archives

The full power of even currently available AI systems can hardly be imagined. Not a single day has passed over the last couple of years when I didn't hear about the discovery of some new and madly creative way of using the tools. But from my perspective—at this point in history at least—the greatest potential lies in a generative AI's ability to instantly read, digest, organize, and then explain vast volumes of raw data.

Large organizations spend millions of dollars building and maintaining systems for managing, parsing, and monitoring the terabytes of data their operations regularly spit out at them. Database managers and security analysts don't come cheap. But what choice do those organizations have? Why generate all that data in the first place if there's no way to properly understand it?

But what about those of us who work for organizations that aren't named Google, Amazon, or Government of . . . ? Our devices and digital activities are probably producing their own data that would love to be read. Well, we may not be able to afford our own teams of database managers, security analysts, or data analysts, but we do have plenty of data. And the age of LLMs is officially upon us.

The trick is to connect our data to a friendly AI. How will we do that? That could be ChatGPT Plus, which lets you upload documents directly. But if it's API access we're after, we could go with the LlamaIndex project (https://gpt-index.readthedocs.io/en/latest/), which we've already seen in chapter 3. LlamaIndex maintains the open source GPTSimpleVectorIndex module along with a full ecosystem of resources for exposing your own data to GPT.

You can read the full documentation guide on LlamaIndex's Read the Docs site (https://mng.bz/oejv). But here's the quick-and-dirty version that'll demonstrate how it works in a Python environment.

The odds are good that you already have the Python programming language installed, along with the Python package manager, `pip`. You can confirm that's the case by running these two commands from your command line. Here's how those looked when I ran them:

```
$ python --version
Python 3.10.12
$ pip --version
pip 22.0.2 from /usr/lib/python3/dist-packages/pip (python 3.10)
```

If your system isn't ready yet, you should head over to appendix C on installing Python at the end of this book. Once everything's in place, we'll install the two modules (`os` and `llama-index`) we'll need for this particular project:

```
pip install os llama-index
```

> **Pro tip!**
> The first troubleshooting step if a `llama-index` operation ever fails is to make sure you've got the latest version installed. You can do that with this command:
> ```
> pip install llama-index –upgrade
> ```

Now we'll start writing our Python code. You'll begin by setting up your GPT-enabled environment by importing the `os` module and adding your OpenAI key. Since LlamaIndex uses the public OpenAI API, nothing will happen without this:

```
import os
os.environ['OPENAI_API_KEY'] = "Your_Key"
```

If you don't yet have a valid OpenAI API key, head over to the API reference page (https://platform.openai.com/docs/api-reference) and click the Sign Up button.

This next code will import the modules that'll do all the heavy lifting. `pathlib` will make it easy for our code to find the location on our local file system where we've saved our data, `GPTVectorStoreIndex` handles the embeddings representing our data that will be generated by `llama_index`, and `download_loader` handles the loader file we'll be working with:

```
from pathlib import Path
from llama_index import GPTVectorStoreIndex
from llama_index import download_loader
```

To keep things simple, you should copy all the documents you want GPT to analyze to a directory beneath the directory where your Python code is running. I chose to call my directory `data`, but you can use whatever you'd prefer. For this example, I downloaded a CSV file from the Kaggle site (https://www.kaggle.com/) containing population numbers for each of the world's nations. I used the dataset found at https://mng.bz/2KDm, although I renamed it `population.csv`.

This code will read the `population.csv` file for a variable called `documents` and then use that data to build a GPT-friendly index that'll take the name `index`:

```
SimpleCSVReader = download_loader("SimpleCSVReader")
loader = SimpleCSVReader(encoding="utf-8")
documents = loader.load_data(file=Path('./data/population.csv'))

index = GPTVectorStoreIndex.from_documents(documents)
```

I'll then submit my query as an argument for the `query_engine.query` method. Just to demonstrate that GPT understands both the CSV (comma-separated values) data and the question I'm asking, I'll ask it for the population of Canada as of 2010. Note that my prompt includes instructions for the LLM on what kind of data the `pop2010` column contains. This will greatly increase the chances it'll understand how to answer my questions:

```
query_engine = index.as_query_engine()
response = query_engine.query("Given that the column with the \
    header `pop2010` contains country population data for the \
    year 2010, what was Canada's population in 2010")
print(response)
```

The response was correct, although the commas were a bit weird:

```
Canada's population in 2010 was 3,396,341,2
```

Let's run one more request. Sticking with the `pop2010` column, I want to know which country's population was, in 2010, the closest to the median population for all countries:

```
query_engine = index.as_query_engine()
response = query_engine.query("Given that the column with the \
    header `pop2010` contains country population data for the \
    year 2010, which country in 2010 had the population that \
    was closest to the median of all countries?")
print(response)
```

Here's what came back:

```
Poland had the population closest to the median of all countries in
2010, with 38,597,353 people.
```

Well, Poland's 2010 population was 38,597,353, but the actual median population of all countries was over 49 million, which meant that Myanmar was the closest. To be fair, Myanmar was only eight spots off from Poland. And GPT's preference for text analysis over simple math operations is well known, if poorly understood. I'd say that things will only improve with time.

Nevertheless, here's another example of an LLM that seems to understand what we're after but doesn't get the job done quite right. And, of course, it's a healthy reminder to always manually confirm that what you're getting from your AI makes real-world sense.

Dig around and you'll find much more to the LllamaIndex project. For instance, the Llama Hub (https://llamahub.ai/) is an archive of "loaders" containing code snippets you can use to connect Llama to your own data. It's maintained within any one of hundreds of popular frameworks, including Wikipedia, Trello, Reddit, and Jira. Those loaders simplify the process of giving GPT access to real-world data in a wide range of environments.

This is about way more than just summarizing stand-alone spreadsheets. Bearing in mind the use-case scenarios I listed at the start of this chapter, just imagine how tools like this can be put to work aggregating data in multiple formats and then mining the data for deep insights.

Seeding a chat session with private data (ChatPDF)

Let me give you an example of just how much better GPT is when working with text than with numbers, at least so far. We're going to take advantage of one of the countless businesses that are rushing to offer value-added GPT-based services. ChatPDF provides a browser-based interface to which you can upload and "chat with" any PDF document.

Just point your browser to https://www.chatpdf.com/, drag your PDF document to the box labeled Drop PDF Here, as shown in figure 5.1, and start asking questions. It works just like a ChatGPT session.

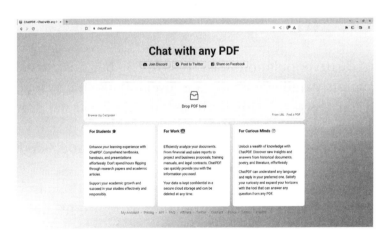

Figure 5.1.   The ChatPDF webpage

But where's the fun in that? Instead, there's no reason why you shouldn't automate and integrate your prompts into sophisticated and efficient scripts. To do that, you'll need to request an API key from ChatPDF using the dialog box that appears when you click the

API link at the bottom of the page. If you get access, you'll be all set for some serious scripting.

The ChatPDF API documentation (https://www.chatpdf.com/docs/api/backend)—at least in its current iteration—provides code snippets for Node.js, Python, and `curl` requests. For this example, I'm going to use the `curl` command-line data transfer tool that we saw in chapter 2.

In our case, sending API requests using `curl` will take two steps, which means you'll run two variations of the `curl` command. Figure 5.2 illustrates the process.

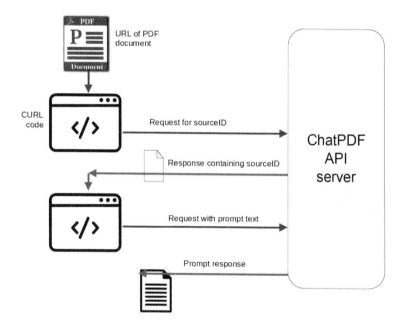

Figure 5.2. **The request/response process using the ChatPDF API**

Here's how that first step will work:

- Authenticate with the ChatPDF API server using the POST method that points to the ChatPDF API address,
- Include the `-H` argument containing your API key (insert in place of the `sec_xxxxxx` dummy code).

- Include the `-d` argument to pass the URL where ChatPDF can find the PDF document you want to query.

And here's the actual code:

```
curl -X POST 'https://api.chatpdf.com/v1/sources/add-url' \
    -H 'x-api-key: sec_xxxxxx' \
    -H 'Content-Type: application/json' \
    -d '{"url": \
       "https://bootstrap-it.com/slidedeck_lpi_security.pdf"}'
```

That URL in my sample code points to a real PDF document, by the way. It's just some slides from a video course on the LPI Security Essentials certification (https://mng.bz/1Gqn) that I recently published. However, since that document doesn't have all that much text in it, you might want to substitute it for your own PDF.

> **NOTE** You could also have run that command as a single line, but formatting it over multiple lines makes it much easier to read. In Bash shell sessions, make sure that the \ backslash at the end of each line (which tells the interpreter that the command continues on to the next line) is the last character on that line. Even an invisible space character will mess everything up.

If that command is successful, it'll return a `sourceID` value, which is the session identifier you'll use going forward when you want to query your PDF. You'll paste that identifier into the second `curl` command. In this example, we use the `-d` argument to send a question ("What is the main topic of this document?"):

```
curl -X POST 'https://api.chatpdf.com/v1/chats/message' \
    -H 'x-api-key: sec_xxxxxx' \
    -H 'Content-Type: application/json' \
    -d '{"sourceId": "src_xxxxx", "messages": [{"role": "user", \
    "content": "What is the main topic of this document?"}]}'
```

Here's the response I got back:

{"content":"The main topic of this document is not specified on the given pages. However, based on the topics listed on page 50, it appears to be related to networking protocols, routing, risk categories, and best practices."}

Here's a more complex example based on something I did recently. It was all about solving a long-standing personal problem that's caused me suffering for three decades now. You see, I've always hated having to come up with assessment questions. This was true during those years when I taught high school, and it's even more true now.

AI to the rescue! Why not convert the transcript for the new video course I'm creating to a single PDF document and see what Chat-PDF has to say about it?

Consider it done. I seeded ChatPDF with that new PDF document exactly the way I showed you earlier. But the request itself is a bit more complicated. You see, I need to make sure that I get assessment questions that address all the course topics and that they comply with some basic formatting needs.

I'll have to create a Bash script that will send the ChatPDF API individual prompts for each set of course topics and then append the output to a file. Figure 5.3 should help you visualize what we're doing here.

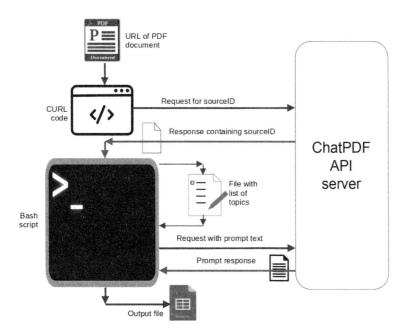

Figure 5.3.   Process for feeding the ChatPDF API with unique, topic-informed requests

To solve the first problem, I created a single text file containing a list of all the course topics, with about four or five topics per line. I then created a Bash script that would expect to be run with the name of that text file as the single argument. Running the script from the command line would look something like this:

```
$ my_script.sh myfile.txt
```

Now here's the script itself:

```
# Read the file line by line
while IFS= read -r line; do
  # Construct the command using a heredoc
  command=$(cat <<EOF
    curl -X POST 'https://api.chatpdf.com/v1/chats/message' \
      -H 'x-api-key: sec_xxxxxx' \
      -H 'Content-Type: application/json' \
      -d '{
        "sourceId": "src_xxxxxx",
        "messages": [
          {
            "role": "user",
            "content": "Based on the information in the PDF file at \
            https://bootstrap-it.com/[...].pdf, create multi-select \
            assessment questions that include the question, five \
            possible answers, the correct answers (identified only \
            by number), and an explanation. The questions should \
            cover each of these topics: $line"
          }
        ]
      }' >> multi_select_raw
EOF
  )

  echo "Executing: $command"
  eval "$command"
done < "$1"
```

Let's break that down into steps. Since the `curl` command is so complicated, the script will iterate through all the lines of the text file as part of a `while` loop:

```
while IFS= read -r line; do
```

For each iteration, it will execute our `curl` command within a `heredoc` format (`$(cat <<EOF…`).

The `content` argument within the `curl` command lays out how I'd like the assessments formatted by ChatPDF:

```
"content": "Based on the information in the PDF file at \
    https://bootstrap-it.com/[...].pdf, create...
```

By the way, I didn't include the actual URL for the PDF; you'll have to pay for the course yourself!

Finally, the script will append (`>> multi_select_raw`) the assessments that come back with each iteration to a file called `multi_select_raw`. The output came in JSON format, which required a bit of manipulation to get it into the shape I wanted. But I guess that's why they pay me the big bucks.

Come to think of it, I could probably have used GPT in one form or another to do the formatting for me. See whether you can figure that out for yourself.

> **Takeaway**
>
> You're not limited to the context provided within short chat prompts: use tools like `llama_index` and ChatPDF (including its API) to train LLMs on as much source material as you need to get informed responses to your requests.

Connecting your AI to the internet (Auto-GPT)

Our final stop in this chapter will be the big, bad internet itself. That's right. We're going to find out whether GPT is better at wasting valuable time watching cute kitten videos than we are. Also, we'll see whether giving a very smart generative AI model access to all the world's knowledge can deliver something valuable in return.

We're going to use the popular Auto-GPT project's Python code provided through a GitHub account called `Significant Gravitas` (https://github.com/Significant-Gravitas/Auto-GPT).

> **NOTE** Git, in case you haven't yet been formally introduced, is a decentralized version control system that tracks changes to files in software projects. It allows multiple developers to collaborate, work on different features simultaneously, and merge their changes seamlessly. It provides a complete history of the project, facilitates code reviews, and enables efficient collaboration in both small- and large-scale software development projects. GitHub is a web-based platform for version control and collaboration, built on top of Git. It provides a centralized hub

for hosting repositories, managing code, and facilitating collaboration among developers.

In the unlikely event you don't yet have Git installed, you can find excellent guides (https://github.com/git-guides/install-git/) in many places. Once that's behind you, run the following `git clone` command to download and unpack the Auto-GPT software:

```
git clone -b \
    stable https://github.com/Significant-Gravitas/Auto-GPT.git
```

For a minimal configuration that'll be good enough for many operations, you'll move into the `AutoGPT` directory that the `git clone` command created and edit a hidden file called `.env.template`. The problem is that the precise location of that directory within the archive keeps changing. Right now, it's a few levels down in `/AutoGPT/autogpts/autogpt`.

When you do get there, look for a line in the `.env.template` file containing the text `OPENAI_API_KEY=`. Make sure that line is uncommented (i.e., that there's no # at the start) and then add your OpenAI API key. Finally, change the name of the saved `.env.template` file to just `.env` (i.e., remove the `.template` extension).

With that, you're all ready to go. Although there are many configuration settings you can play with to tweak performance. You'll find configuration files in the root (`Auto-GPT`) directory and in the `autogpt` directory that's below it. Keep in mind the details about settings like, for instance, `Temperature`, that you already learned about in chapter 2. There may (or may not) be a file called `prompt_settings.yaml` where you can set default prompt settings.

Here's how that file will, by default, look:

```
constraints: [
   'Exclusively use the commands listed below.',
   'You can only act proactively, and are unable to start background jobs
or set up webhooks for yourself. Take this into account when planning
your actions.',
   'You are unable to interact with physical objects. If this is
absolutely necessary to fulfill a task or objective or to complete a
step, you must ask the user to do it for you. If the user refuses this,
and there is no other way to achieve your goals, you must terminate to
avoid wasting time and energy.'
]
resources: [
   'Internet access for searches and information gathering.',
```

```
 'The ability to read and write files.',
 'You are a Large Language Model, trained on millions of pages of text,
including a lot of factual knowledge. Make use of this factual knowledge
to avoid unnecessary gathering of information.'
]
best_practices: [
 'Continuously review and analyze your actions to ensure you are
performing to the best of your abilities.',
 'Constructively self-criticize your big-picture behavior constantly.',
 'Reflect on past decisions and strategies to refine your approach.',
 'Every command has a cost, so be smart and efficient. Aim to complete
tasks in the least number of steps.',
 'Only make use of your information gathering abilities to find
information that you don''t yet have knowledge of.'
```

Feel free to edit that file so it more closely matches your needs.

Fully configuring and then launching AutoGPT can be as simple as running the `autogpt.sh` or `autogpt.bat` file. But you might want to consult the `run.sh` or `run.bat` files in the `Auto-GPT` directory for alternatives. And, as always, the official documentation (https://docs.agpt.co/) is going to be helpful.

When AutoGPT launches, you'll (probably) be asked whether you want to reload a previous session's settings (which, if this is your first time using the program, would be the preset default) or whether you'd prefer to start something new. If you go with something new, you'll be asked for an AI name, a description of the role you want this AI to play, and then up to five goals—although I've seen the process change so many times between versions that I really can't say what you'll end up seeing. But stability and predictability aren't attributes that get along well with AI, are they?

Once you've entered your goals, AutoGPT will head off to figure out how it should solve the problem and come back with its thinking and recommendations. AutoGPT is verbose. It'll tell you what it thinks about the task you've given it, what potential problems it might face, and how it might be able to solve those problems. It'll also present a multistep plan of action. All those discussions will, by default, be saved to a JSON-formatted file in the `AutoGPT` directory called `auto-gpt.json`.

By default, it'll wait for you to approve each new next step of its plan. Alternatively, although there is some risk involved, you can give it permission to perform, say, the next 10 steps without asking permission by responding with something like the following:

```
Input: y -10
```

I should note that the process I'm going to describe did end up costing me around $3.00 in OpenAI API costs.

So let's see what we can do here. I recently used the tool for some serious research for my business. I've been debating whether I should create a book and course covering the objectives of a relatively new technology certification. My doubts center around the question of whether there will be enough demand from students planning to earn the certification to make my new content useful.

I asked AutoGPT to use the internet to rank the popularity of this particular certification against a couple of other older certs (whose value I'm in a better position to gauge). Here, in slightly modified form, is how I framed my request:

 AI Name: Assess popularity of [...] certifications Description: Assess the relative popularity of the [...] certifications to know which one might be the most profitable for a new certification study guide course Goal 1: Compare the popularity of following certification programs: [...]. Goal 2: Estimate the likely future demand for each of the certification programs among potential students. Goal 3: Estimate the likely demand for training programs (like Udemy courses, books) for each certification programs. Goal 4: Estimate each certification's popularity using a scale of 0 - 100 and save the results to a local file. Goal 5: Shut down.

After around 4 hours(!) of independently thinking, browsing, and searching, AutoGPT gave me a file that ranked three certifications—including the new one I'm considering—by scores between 0 and 100. For context, I copied the enormous raw output it generated (there was nearly 200K of it) and converted it to a PDF. I then uploaded that PDF to ChatPDF to try to discover more about the methodology.

After all the dust had settled, I was actually impressed with the results. Based on AutoGPT's in-process output, it seems to have used a wide range of online resources, including social media discussions, Amazon reviews, and content nested deeply within the web sites of various related organizations. Those 4 hours did seem to stretch on, but I'm happy with what that bought me.

Having said that, AutoGPT can sometimes lose its way. The most common (and frustrating) problem I've faced is its tendency to fail with the same futile operation over and over again. At this point, if the agent is just going round and round in circles, your best bet is to simply shut it down.

And while we're on the subject of giving LLMs internet access, the regular ChatGPT can, from time to time, be convinced to access live internet URLs, although it's been known to get cranky when it's just not in the mood. ChatGPT Plus is far more easygoing on that front.

Try this for yourself

Identify a PDF file containing, say, the many objectives for an IT-related certification program—something like the AWS Certified Cloud Practitioner (https://mng.bz/PZzv) perhaps:

- Feed the PDF to both ChatPDF and LlamaIndex and ask for a detailed summary of the exam objectives.
- Compare the results you get.
- Ask AutoGPT for a summary of that certification's objectives.

Do humans come with built-in USB-C ports?

Summary

- We used the `GPTVectorStoreIndex` from LlamaIndex to get GPT to read and analyze locally hosted data, which can include CSV and PDF files (among others).
- We used ChatPDF to assess and query our own PDF documents, both through the web interface and, programmatically, through the ChatPDF API.
- We used AutoGPT to create a GPT-fueled agent capable of searching the live internet for data of all kinds to answer complex sequences of questions.

Prompt engineering: Optimizing your experience 6

This chapter covers

- The definition of prompt engineering
- Prompt engineering best practices
- Zero-shot and few-shot prompting
- Prompting LLMs for historical time-series datasets

I'll bet that before actually opening this book, many—perhaps most—of you expected *prompt engineering* to be a primary focus. And yet, here we are in chapter 6 (halfway through the book!), and we're only just hitting the topic. What's the story here?

In my defense, I'd say that it's partly about what we mean when we use the term. For some, prompt engineering covers a lot of what you'll figure out on your own by just having fun experimenting with ChatGPT or MidJourney. It matters, but it doesn't require a whole book.

But I'd also argue that what I've given you so far—and what's yet to come in the remaining chapters—goes far beyond prompts. Sure, the phrasing you use is important, but the API and programmatic tools we're discovering will take your prompts a lot further.

There's one more thing going on. In my experience, as GPT and other generative AI models improve, they're getting better at figuring out what you want, even when you provide a weak prompt. I can't count the number of times that GPT has successfully seen right through my spelling and grammar errors, poor wording, or sometimes even outright technical mistakes. So, many of the problems that popular prompt engineering advice seeks to prevent are already easily handled by the AI itself.

Still, no one wants to look like an idiot, even if the only one who will notice is a robot. And you can never know when even an AI won't be able to figure out what you're really after. So I'll devote this entire chapter to the fine art of engineering your prompts. We'll finish up with a full-stack demo that'll include a guide to visualizing the data your prompt generates. But we'll begin with a helpful definition.

What is prompt engineering?

Prompt engineering is a technique used in the context of language models like GPT to effectively guide the model's responses and improve its performance. It involves crafting specific instructions or queries, known as prompts, to encourage (or even force) a desired output from the model.

Prompt engineering can be used to shape the behavior of the model by providing it with explicit instructions, context, or constraints. By carefully constructing prompts, researchers and developers can influence the model's output and make it more consistent, accurate, or better aligned with specific criteria.

There are various strategies for prompt engineering, depending on what you're trying to accomplish. These strategies may involve

- Asking the model to assume a particular role ("You are an expert investment counselor.")
- Specifying the format you'd like for the model's response ("Give me the response in .CSV format.")

- Asking the model to think step by step ("Can you walk me through the process of installing software package X, step by step?")
- Providing additional context or background information ("This assumes that the value for the variable `my_number` is 10.")
- Using system messages (like error messages) to guide the model's behavior

One common technique is to use *prompt engineering by demonstration,* where developers manually generate desired model outputs for a set of example inputs. The model is then fine-tuned based on this data, allowing it to generalize and produce similar responses for future inputs.

It's important to keep in mind that prompt engineering is an *iterative process.* That means you don't always expect to get the completion you're after on the first try. Instead, you'll experiment, analyze the model's initial behavior, and refine subsequent prompts based on feedback and evaluation. The process of gradual iteration lets you use the power of language models while maintaining control over the output and ensuring it aligns with your intentions and requirements.

For one example, you might want to use iterative prompting when your large language model (LLM) gives you programming code that doesn't work. Rather than starting over by asking the same question a second time, you could copy and paste any error message you received and ask how that could be avoided.

Prompt engineering best practices

These suggestions are based on guidance found in the official OpenAI documentation (https://mng.bz/X1O1).

Be specific

Be generous with the details and descriptions you include in your prompt. Compare the following two prompts:

 Tell me about quantum mechanics.

DA Explain quantum mechanics in 200 words or less and in terms that can be understood by a 12-year-old.

The first prompt won't be as effective as the second prompt. Similarly, compare the next two prompts:

DA Compose an email to my boss asking for a raise.

DA Compose a polite but forceful email to my boss explaining how my hard work and successfully executed, on-time projects have earned the company new clients.

The first prompt is a lot less likely to end happily than something like the second prompt.

Be clear

The more obvious and unambiguous you can make your prompt, the less chance you'll get something unexpected. This example isn't necessarily bad:

DA Considering the data provided, list all the key topics, arguments, and people that are referenced.

But you're far more likely to achieve success the first time around using something like this:

DA Considering the data provided, list all the key topics that are referenced, then the arguments that are presented, and, finally, each of the people who are mentioned.
Desired format: Topics: <list_divided _by_commas>
Arguments: People:

Avoid unnecessary words

There's a higher risk of misunderstanding and poor completion results when you use this kind of overly verbose prompt:

DA I'm looking for a fairly long and completely detailed description of each of the ten most popular passenger cars of the early 1970s (by domestic US sales).

Instead, try something like this:

 List and describe each of the ten highest selling cars in the US during the early 1970s.

When I ran both the extra verbose and sleek and punchy versions past ChatGPT, the results I got were equally impressive. So I'd say this is a good illustration of GPT improvements I mentioned earlier. It's also an indication of the growing irrelevance of the topic of prompt engineering as a whole.

Separate reference text from your instructions

You should make it clear where your instructions end and any reference text you're including begins. This example might not work:

 Who was the author of: We can only see a short distance ahead, but we can see plenty there that needs to be done.

But this probably will (note the use of triple quotations, although I'm not sure that they're still as important as they once were):

 Who was the author of the following text:

Text: """"We can only see a short distance ahead, but we can see plenty there that needs to be done.""""

By the way, as I'm sure you're curious, the author was Alan Turing.

Be positive, not negative

This works in personal relationships too. But right now we're more concerned with the way you get along with your favorite generative AI. It seems that GPT and its cousins can sometimes get confused by negatives like this:

 When responding to the following request for help from a customer who is locked out of their account, DO NOT suggest they update their password.

Rephrasing the prompt as a positive might make a difference:

When responding to the following request for help from a customer who is locked out of their account, instead of suggesting they update their password, refer them to available online documentation.

There are a few other LLM training methods that can be applied in the specific context of prompts to improve the quality of your completions. We'll look at those next.

Takeaway

When composing your prompts, remember to be specific, clear, concise, and positive and to clearly demarcate your reference text.

Control for temperature (randomness)

You can directly incorporate temperature within a prompt:

 Generate a creative and unique story beginning with the sentence "It was a dark and stormy night." Use a temperature setting of 0.8 to add some randomness and creativity to the story.

In this example, the temperature setting of 0.8 indicates that the generated response will have a moderate level of randomness and creativity. The higher the temperature, the more varied and unpredictable the output will be. You can adjust the temperature value to control the amount of randomness in the generated text. A higher value like 0.8 will result in more diverse and imaginative responses, while a lower value like 0.2 will produce more focused and deterministic responses.

Zero-shot and few-shot prompting

Zero-shot and few-shot prompting are techniques used in natural language processing (NLP) to generate responses or perform tasks without explicit training on specific examples or with only a limited amount of training data.

Zero-shot prompting refers to the ability of a model to provide meaningful responses or perform tasks for which it has not been explicitly trained. The model is capable of generalizing from its training data to understand and respond to new inputs or tasks. This is achieved by using prompts or instructions that guide the model's behavior. For example, if a language model has been trained on a variety of topics, it can still generate coherent responses on a new topic by providing a prompt that specifies the desired topic.

Few-shot prompting, on the other hand, involves training a model with only a small amount of labeled data or examples. By using this limited training data, the model is expected to learn how to generalize and perform tasks on unseen or novel examples. This approach is useful when the availability of labeled data is scarce or when adapting a model to new tasks quickly.

Both zero-shot and few-shot prompting use the pretraining and fine-tuning methodology. In pretraining, a model is trained on a large corpus of text data to learn general language patterns and representations. Fine-tuning follows, where the pretrained model is further trained on specific tasks or domains using limited labeled data or prompts. This combination enables the model to exhibit adaptability and generate meaningful responses or perform tasks in a zero-shot or few-shot manner. These techniques have proven to be powerful in various NLP tasks, such as

- Text classification
- Question answering
- Summarization
- Language translation
- Text generation

They allow models to demonstrate a degree of understanding and perform adequately on new or unseen inputs, even without extensive training on specific examples.

Here's an example of zero-shot prompting. Let's say you have a language model that has been trained on a variety of topics but hasn't been explicitly trained on the topic of space exploration. Using zero-shot prompting, you can still generate coherent responses to space-related questions. For example, you could provide the following prompt:

What are the key challenges and achievements in space exploration?

The model, even without specific training on space exploration, can generate a response by drawing upon its general knowledge and understanding of the topic.

And here's an example of few-shot prompting. Suppose you have a model that has been pretrained on a large corpus of text but hasn't been fine-tuned for sentiment analysis. However, with few-shot prompting, you can train the model on a small labeled dataset containing a few examples of positive and negative sentiments. The model can then generalize from this limited training data and perform sentiment analysis on new, unseen text.

Here's a more generic example of how a few-shot prompt might look. We would first train the model using these prompt/completion examples:

 English sentence: "I love to travel."

French translation: "J'adore voyager."

English sentence: "The cat is sleeping."

French translation: "Le chat dort."

English sentence: "Where is the nearest train station?"

French translation: "Où se trouve la gare la plus proche?"

At this point, you've "trained" the model to anticipate the kind of result you want. You're now ready to submit an actual prompt:

 English sentence "Can you recommend a good restaurant?"

French translation:

Both zero-shot and few-shot prompting use the model's ability to generalize from its pretraining and make predictions or perform tasks on new inputs or tasks, either with minimal or no specific training. They're fundamental tools used by AI engineers when they design their LLMs, but the same basic principles can also be used for our own day-to-day AI interactions.

Prompt for time-series data: A practical example

When you know someone who happens to have perfect command of the entire internet, creating new value from your relationship is often just a matter of being creative enough to ask the right questions. As one does, I recently had an irrepressible urge to visualize historical improvements in server hardware components. Has capacity growth been consistent over the years? Has capacity grown at similar rates for all component categories?

But where would I find the data? My curiosity wasn't irrepressible enough to justify scouring archived versions of vendor websites for hours on end. Could my smart "friend" (by which I mean GPT or one of its LLM cousins) help me out here? No reason not to try. Here's my prompt:

 Give me the basic specifications for out-of-the-box, top-of-the-line rack-mount servers from each year between 1994 and 2021. Show me the output in CSV format using the following columns: Year, clock speed (GHz), Maximum RAM (GB), Total Drive Capacity (GB).

Since I expected to load the output into a Python program, I figured I'd save myself some work and ask for the data in comma-separated values (CSV) format using exactly the column headers I preferred. I tried this out using both ChatGPT and Perplexity Labs' LLM server (https://labs.perplexity.ai/). To my astonishment, GPT gave me nicely formatted CSV data that at least looked realistic. For some reason, Perplexity interpreted "CSV" as "Markdown," but fixing that wasn't a big deal.

The data itself (along with the code used in the following examples) are available as part of the book's GitHub repo (https://mng .bz/y8wo).

Visualizing the data

Of course, properly visualizing my data will be essential for assessing whether the output makes sense and, if it does, what insights it might give me. But, as I'll show you, how you visualize this data will determine how well you'll understand it. Let me explain that by showing you how to generate charts using both normalized and non-normalized data.

Normalization refers to the process of adjusting data values to a common scale or standard, typically to facilitate meaningful comparisons between different data points. It's a common technique used in data visualization and analysis to remove the influence of varying scales or units in the data, making it easier to identify patterns and trends. In our case, that's important because the scale of the units used to measure CPU clock speeds (GHz) is very different from the units used to measure memory (GB) and storage (also GB).

Normalization helps ensure that the relative relationships and variations within the data are preserved while removing the influence of different scales. This is especially useful when comparing data from different sources or when visualizing data on the same graph with different units or scales.

Min–max scaling, also known as min–max normalization, is a data normalization method used to transform data into a specific range, typically between 0 and 1. The purpose of min–max scaling is to standardize data values, making them more comparable and suitable for various data analysis and machine learning techniques.

Here's how min–max scaling works:

1. Find the minimum (min) and maximum (max) values within the dataset for the feature you want to normalize.
2. For each data point in that feature, apply the following formula to scale it to the range [0, 1]: Scaled Value = (Original Value - Min) / (Max - Min).

The resulting scaled value for each data point will fall within the range of 0 to 1, where 0 represents the minimum value in the dataset, and 1 represents the maximum value.

Min–max scaling is particularly useful when you want to preserve the relationships and proportions between data points while ensuring that all values are on a consistent scale. It's widely used in various data analysis and machine learning tasks, especially when algorithms like neural networks, k-means clustering, or support vector machines are sensitive to the scale of input features.

To illustrate, suppose you have a dataset that represents the employee salaries ranging from $40,000 to $100,000. You also have data representing the number of years of experience each employee has, ranging from 2 to 20 years. You want to standardize these values using min–max scaling.

Without min–max scaling, the salary values could range from 40,000 to 100,000, while the years of experience could range from 2 to 20. The data points for salary and years of experience would be on very different scales.

Now, if you apply min–max scaling to both features, you might scale the values to a range of 0 to 1. So, a salary of $50,000 could be scaled to 0.25, and 10 years of experience might be scaled to 0.5.

Min–max scaling is the tool we'll use here. But first, I'll show you what we get using non-normalized data for a graph so you'll see with your own eyes why normalization can be helpful.

Graphing the time-series data without normalization

Listing 6.1 shows the complete code for producing a non-normalized graph of our data. Look through it yourself and try to understand what's happening, and then we'll work through it one section at a time.

Listing 6.1 Visualizing a time-series without normalization

```
import pandas as pd
from matplotlib import pyplot as plt

df_all = pd.read_csv('AllServers.csv')

plt.figure(figsize=(10, 6))                              ◀——— Sets the figure size


years = df_all['Year'].to_numpy()                                    Converts
clock_speed = df_all['Clock Speed (GHz)'].to_numpy()                 DataFrame
max_ram = df_all['Maximum RAM (GB)'].to_numpy()                      columns to
drive_capacity = df_all['Total Drive Capacity (GB)'].to_numpy()      NumPy arrays


plt.plot(years, clock_speed, label='Clock speed (GHz)')       Plots lines for each
plt.plot(years, max_ram, label='RAM (GB)')                    column against the
plt.plot(years, drive_capacity, label='Storage (GB)')         Year column
```

```
plt.xlabel('Year')
plt.ylabel('Values')                                              Sets labels and title
plt.title('System Specifications Over Time')


plt.legend()                                          ◀─────────  Adds a legend


plt.grid(True)
plt.show()                                            ◀─────────  Shows the plot
```

Let's walk through that code. As always, we begin by importing the libraries we'll need. pandas will handle the data itself, and Matplotlib will help us with the graphs. We'll then import the CSV data file into a data frame:

```
import pandas as pd
from matplotlib import pyplot as plt
df_all = pd.read_csv('AllServers.csv')
```

I'll define the dimensions of the graph (or *figure* as it's more commonly described) that I'll eventually generate. By all means, experiment with alternate values to see what changes. But these should be perfectly workable:

```
plt.figure(figsize=(10, 6))  # Set the figure size
```

We'll use the NumPy tool to take each of the columns and convert it to a NumPy array, which is a data format that's usable for plotting our graph/figure. We'll give the array created from the data in each column a name. The column `df_all['Year']`, for instance, will be called `years`:

```
years = df_all['Year'].to_numpy()
clock_speed = df_all['Clock Speed (GHz)'].to_numpy()
max_ram = df_all['Maximum RAM (GB)'].to_numpy()
drive_capacity = df_all['Total Drive Capacity (GB)'].to_numpy()
```

Since `years` will be used as our x-axis, I'll now plot the other three NumPy arrays. Each of those arrays will be associated with the `years` values and given a display label like `label='Clock speed (GHz)'`:

```
plt.plot(years, clock_speed, label='Clock speed (GHz)')
plt.plot(years, max_ram, label='RAM (GB)')
plt.plot(years, drive_capacity, label='Storage (GB)')
```

To make the graph more readable, we'll add labels to both the x and y axes and give the figure itself a title. We'll also add a color-coded legend so we'll be able to quickly understand which plot line represents which column of data:

```
plt.xlabel('Year')
plt.ylabel('Values')
plt.title('System Specifications Over Time')

plt.legend()
```

Finally, we'll pull the trigger and generate the figure itself:

```
plt.grid(True)
plt.show()
```

Figure 6.1 shows how it'll all come out.

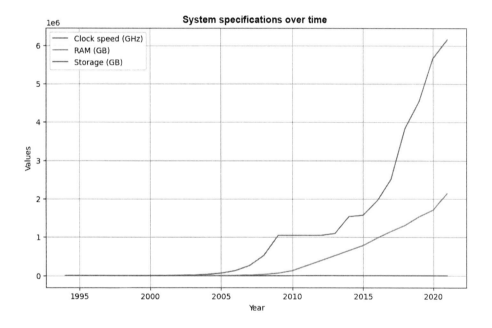

Figure 6.1. **Our hardware component data visualized using non-normalized data**

Besides the fact that it won't be easy for those of you reading this in a physical book to distinguish between the color-coded plot lines, there's another, more serious, problem here. A casual glance would lead us to conclude that processor clock speeds haven't improved at all in the years since 1994. But that's ridiculous.

The data itself shows average clock speeds going from 1 GHz to 11 GHz over that time. That last number (11) is weird. I'm aware of no processor on earth that can run at 11 GHz. I suspect that the Perplexity LLM is accounting for the spread of multicore systems and simply adding the maximum speeds of each parallel core that might be installed on a system. But in any case, why does that growth not show up in our plotline?

The answer is that the difference between 1 GHz and 11 GHz isn't anything like the difference between 32 GB and 6,144,960 GB. It's all about *scale*. To fix that, we'll need to normalize our data.

Graphing the time-series data with normalization

You'll immediately notice that the code in listing 6.2 is significantly different from the non-normalization example just before. The first difference is that we're importing the `MinMaxScaler` module from the `sclikit-learn` library. Look through the whole thing, and then we'll work through the rest of the code section by section.

Listing 6.2   Visualizing a time series with normalization

```
import pandas as pd
from matplotlib import pyplot as plt
from sklearn.preprocessing import MinMaxScaler

df_servers = pd.read_csv("AllServers.csv")


years = df_servers['Year'].values
scaler = MinMaxScaler()
normalized_data = scaler.fit_transform\
    (df_servers.drop(columns=['Year']))


plt.figure(figsize=(10, 6))


for i, column_name in enumerate(df_servers.columns[1:]):
    plt.plot(years, normalized_data[:, i], label=column_name)


plt.xlabel('Year')
plt.ylabel('Normalized Values')
plt.title('"All Servers" (Normalized) Specs Over Time')


plt.legend()
```

Extracts the Year column and normalizes the other columns

Plots the normalized data using matplotlib

Plots for each normalized column against the Year column

Sets labels and title

Adds a legend

```
plt.grid(True)
plt.show()                                    ◀──────── Shows the plot
```

We extract the data from the `Year` column the same way we did earlier. Those values will work just fine as they are. But then we'll normalize the other columns of data by applying the `MinMaxScaler` module (identified as `scaler`). We'll assign the magically transformed data to the variable `normalized_data`:

```
years = df_servers['Year'].values
scaler = MinMaxScaler()
normalized_data = scaler.fit_transform\
        (df_servers.drop(columns=['Year']))
```

We'll then cycle through each column of data (`for i, column_name`) and plot their data against the `years` data. This data is then generated (`plt.plot`). The `label=column_name` argument applies the existing names for each of the three regular data columns to the normalized data we're generating:

```
for i, column_name in enumerate(df_servers.columns[1:]):
    plt.plot(years, normalized_data[:, i], label=column_name)
```

Finally, as before, we set the labels and title, add a legend, and then generate the figure itself. Figure 6.2 shows how that looks.

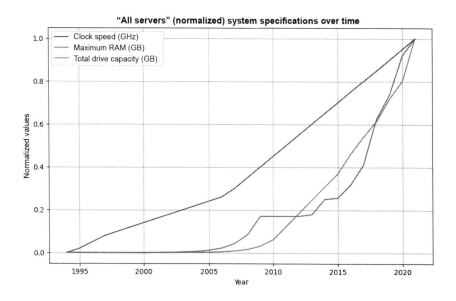

Figure 6.2.   Our hardware component data visualized using normalized data

That's a huge improvement. We can see relatively steady growth trends for all three component classes. The thing to remember is that the plotlines normalization gives us are also imperfect. That's because the start and finish values for all three plot lines are set to 0 and 1, respectively. So, by looking at this graph, it'll be impossible to tell whether any one class grew faster than the others. But, given that limitation, we should be able to visually identify any significant trends, like the apparent lack of growth in storage capacity between 2009 and 2013 or so.

I should admit that right before this book went to print, I tried the same original "Give me the basic specifications . . ." prompt on ChatGPT Plus. Not only did it give me better data, but without being asked, it generated a normalized plot that looked pretty much identical to the one in figure 6.2. That was simply way too easy!

Of course, this is AI-generated data, so you shouldn't assume it's all correct. Don't go investing your life savings based on these numbers.

Try this for yourself

Prompt your favorite LLM with a simple one-shot question ("Write me a script for a dialogue between an IT support professional and an inexperienced client," perhaps). Then ask for the same dialogue, but this time, start the request off with a few-shot prefix.

Are you absolutely sure you want to do this?

Summary

- Prompt engineering techniques can be used to precisely guide LLMs to respond to our particular needs.
- Basic prompt engineering best practices include being specific, clear, concise, and positive.
- Few-shot prompts can incorporate examples to teach a model the kinds of results you're looking for.
- LLMs can be prompted for estimates of real-world time-series data and then explore two ways to visualize that data (normalized and non-normalized).

7

Outperforming legacy research and learning tools

This chapter covers

- Generating accurate and reliable investment guidance
- Integrating large language models (LLMs) into your skill-adoption workflow
- Integrating LLMs into your daily work

It's been said that AI won't put anyone out of work, but that people using AI will put people *not* using AI out of work. Assuming, of course, that AI doesn't end up killing us all first, what can we do to ensure we end up in the group of happy users and not the regret-filled outsiders sadly looking in?

Let me give you some context. I'm a lot older than you might think. I wrote my first book on sheets of paper using a pen. It may have been a very old technology, but it was solar-powered (translation: it was only useful when I opened a window or turned the lights on). Granted, I did later painstakingly type out that entire book into a computer. But I did so using sofware (WordPerfect 4.2 for DOS) that didn't even have its own spellchecker.

My publishing career has enjoyed periodic boosts from new technologies ever since: my first printer (a hand-me-down from my brother-in-law), my first document scanner, my first internet connection (yup, that actually came *after* the printer and the scanner), my first DSL modem, my discovery and adoption of Linux, and so on. Each of those changes had a noticeable affect on my productivity and efficiency.

But none of those came close to the nuclear-powered turbo charge I got from generative AI (although, technically, I'm not sure a turbo charge can be nuclear-powered). It's not just the blinding speed with which I can access details about events, relationships, processes, and trends. And it's not just the sheer volume of parsed data that's suddenly available to me. It's that everything is moving so much faster now. Everything I do just happens without lag.

Here are just a few of my interactions from just the past week:

- Once upon a time, choosing a new (previously enjoyed) laptop would require long and deep research: Does the HP EliteBook 840 G3 have all the ports I need? What video chipset does it use? How does its CPU rate against benchmark performance scores of other CPUs I've run? But today, I can just ask "Can you compare the specs and performance of an HP Elitebook 840 G1 laptop with a Lenovo ThinkPad T420?"; and then "Would the G3 with an i5 chip be better than a G1 with an i7 chip?"; and finally, "What kind of battery life can I expect?"

- Once upon a time, figuring out how to access the WiFi radio card on a particular laptop would have involved searching online for copies of the right user manual and searching through the manual hoping that the information was there. Now, I can just ask "How do you access the WiFi card on a Lenovo ThinkPad T420?"

- Once upon a time, getting some background on specific medical issues would have meant diving through online archives of medical studies, hoping someone has actually done the research and that it's been published, it's available online, and you can extract meaning from it in within a reasonable time-frame. Today? Just ask "Would the results of an ECHO (echocardiogram) stress test be altered by the patient wearing a surgical mask (restricting their airflow)?"

Of course, you'll need to remember to confirm whatever information AI gives you—especially medical information. But even so, you'll definitely want a piece of that action. So let me use a few examples to give you a sense of how just about every research task you used to do can now be done better, faster, and more accurately.

Asking for investment guidance

Can GPT pick stock market buys and sells for you? Yes, it can. Can GPT actually execute the transactions without your involvement? Yes. That, too, is possible. Is that a good idea? Perhaps not just yet. To be perfectly honest, I'm not in any mad rush to push that particular start button.

But as we've seen over and over, AI tools have many specific strengths that translate to superpowers when applied to the right problem scenario. Well, I'd say that investment guidance is about as close to a right-problem scenario as you're likely to find.

One obvious reason for this is that making smart investment decisions involves digesting a lot of data. How much data? Just a single Form 10-K report, which publicly traded companies are required to file annually with the US Securities and Exchange Commission (SEC), can contain upward of 100,000 words. And, as a rule, they're not exactly inspired writing. So don't expect one to keep you enraptured through a lazy summer afternoon at the beach.

On the other hand, you can't truly understand a company's current value or accurately anticipate what the future holds without somehow reading and absorbing the fundamentals contained in that 10-K, along with other documents. And don't ignore how the very nature of investment research involves performing this due diligence not only on a single company but on dozens or thousands.

Wouldn't it be wonderful if there were some kind of—oh, I don't know—a digital tool of some sort that could access and analyze all that data for us? D'ya think GPT might be helpful here?

Well, at least for now, forget about ChatGPT: 100,000 words is way too long for a chat prompt. But by this point in the book, you're already familiar with ways around that limitation. So here's what happened when I took Tesla's Form 10-K for fiscal year ending December 31, 2021, and fed it to ChatPDF.

The document itself is available as a web page on the SEC site (https://mng.bz/qOr6). To convert that to a PDF document, I first downloaded the HTML to my computer using `wget`:

```
wget <url>
```

The sheer size of the file gave me some trouble, so I used the Cloud Convert website (https://cloudconvert.com/html-to-md) to convert the file to Markddown. From there, the free file converter program `Pandoc` made it easy to produce a PDF:

```
pandoc -o tesla_10k.pdf --pdf-engine=xelatex tesla_10k.md
```

I dropped that PDF into ChatPDF and gave it the following prompt:

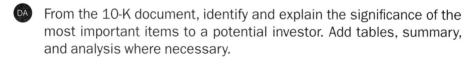

From the 10-K document, identify and explain the significance of the most important items to a potential investor. Add tables, summary, and analysis where necessary.

Here's part of the response I received (the chart was helpfully delivered in Markdown format):

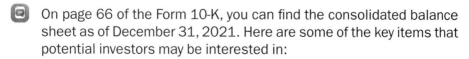

On page 66 of the Form 10-K, you can find the consolidated balance sheet as of December 31, 2021. Here are some of the key items that potential investors may be interested in:

(continued)

Item	Amount (in millions)
Cash and cash equivalents	$16,214
Marketable securities	$9,986
Total current assets	$38,535
Property, plant and equipment, net	$22,936
Total assets	$121,872
Total current liabilities	$23,758
Long-term debt	$12,385
Total liabilities	$63,091
Total stockholders' equity	$58,781

Cash and cash equivalents and marketable securities are important items for potential investors because they represent Tesla's liquidity position. As of December 31, 2021, Tesla had a total of $26.2 billion in cash and marketable securities. This is a significant increase from the previous year's balance of $19.4 billion. This increase in liquidity is a positive sign for investors as it indicates that Tesla has sufficient resources to fund its operations and invest in growth opportunities.

Property, plant and equipment is another important item for investors as it represents Tesla's investment in fixed assets such as factories and equipment. As of December 31, 2021, Tesla had property, plant and equipment with a net book value of $22.9 billion. This represents an increase from the previous year's balance of $18.6 billion which indicates that Tesla has continued to invest heavily in its manufacturing capabilities.

Total liabilities is also an important item for investors as it represents Tesla's debt obligations. As of December 31, 2021, Tesla had total liabilities of $63.1 billion, which includes . . .

To get a fuller picture, you'll probably want to dig deeper with more questions. Here's one I tried:

Is the company's current resource allocation at all risky?

which inspired this response:

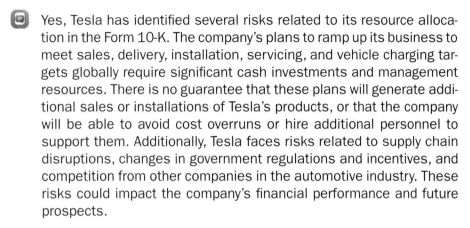

Yes, Tesla has identified several risks related to its resource allocation in the Form 10-K. The company's plans to ramp up its business to meet sales, delivery, installation, servicing, and vehicle charging targets globally require significant cash investments and management resources. There is no guarantee that these plans will generate additional sales or installations of Tesla's products, or that the company will be able to avoid cost overruns or hire additional personnel to support them. Additionally, Tesla faces risks related to supply chain disruptions, changes in government regulations and incentives, and competition from other companies in the automotive industry. These risks could impact the company's financial performance and future prospects.

The next question is something that would be helpful for our research:

 What are Tesla's current ratio and debt-to-equity ratio?

Here's what came back:

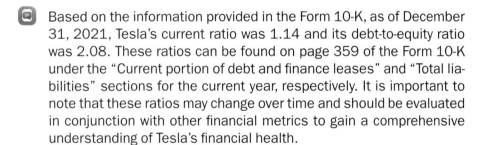

Based on the information provided in the Form 10-K, as of December 31, 2021, Tesla's current ratio was 1.14 and its debt-to-equity ratio was 2.08. These ratios can be found on page 359 of the Form 10-K under the "Current portion of debt and finance leases" and "Total liabilities" sections for the current year, respectively. It is important to note that these ratios may change over time and should be evaluated in conjunction with other financial metrics to gain a comprehensive understanding of Tesla's financial health.

Looking for some context for that? A simple follow-up question can help:

 Can you help me understand the significance of those ratios?

And here's just a little taste of the response I received:

The current ratio is a liquidity ratio that measures a company's ability to pay its short-term obligations using its current assets. A current ratio of 1 or higher is generally considered good, as it indicates that the company has enough current assets to cover its short-term liabilities. In Tesla's case, the current ratio of 1.14 suggests that the company has enough current assets to cover its short-term obligations. . . .

You get the idea. But that's only the beginning. Working through an AI's analysis of each company will still take significant time. But with the API tools we've already encountered in earlier chapters, there's nothing stopping you from putting together a (relatively) simple automated script to

- Download Form 10-K documents for 10, 100, or 1,000 companies.
- Convert the HTML documents to PDFs.
- Submit each PDF to ChatPDF through its API.
- Prompt GPT to assign each company a score based on its assessment of each 10-K.
- Return a list in which all assessed companies are ranked by their scores.

Not sure how to write the script? Ask OpenAI's you-know-who. Just a friendly heads-up: that script will probably stretch into hundreds of lines, and even with the help of your AI, it'll take hours to debug.

Keeping in mind all appropriate API charges, there's also nothing stopping you from running this script every day, week, or month, or from opening your own fully automated market research service (and, a few months later, retiring to the Greek islands in your super yacht).

Sound promising? Well, I can assure you that we're not the first to think of it. For instance, an organization called Global Predictions offers individuals a free service called Portfolio Pilot. The application uses sophisticated AI pipelines to analyze macro market conditions and apply the insights it produces to each user's own portfolio profile. Using (hopefully) solid investment principles, the tool can offer real-time investment advice.

The kicker is that rather than monetizing user engagement through user fees, advertising, or commissions on sales, Portfolio Pilot states that it's "learning with and from users about how to best interact with our economic models, running simulations, and applying insights directly to their portfolios" (https://mng.bz/7dD7). Or, in other words, they're using the value of access to significant volumes of consumer investment data.

Naturally, it's worth repeating that an LLM's guidance (on this or any other topic) is just a computer blindly stringing together 1s and 0s. A computer may be somewhat less likely to knowingly cheat you than a flesh-and-blood stockbroker, but it should still never be trusted blindly. Use the guidance as an important base for informed decisions.

> **Takeaway**
>
> No matter how complicated it might be, any PDF document (containing 120 pages or less) can be submitted to ChatPDF and subjected to a sustained and in-depth interrogation. And, as with any API, ChatPDF interactions can be automated and, therefore, incorporated into sophisticated operations. By the way, you're definitely not limited to English-language documents for any of this.

Connecting search engines to AI using LangChain

As we've already seen, the developer universe has exploded with ingenious new tools, applications, and processes for working with LLMs and generative AI. One particularly versatile example is the LangChain project (https://www.langchain.com/). The overall goal involves providing easy integrations with various LLM models. The LangChain ecosystem is also host to a growing number of (sometimes experimental) projects pushing the limits of the humble LLM.

Spend some time browsing the LangChain website to get a sense of what's possible. You'll see how many tools are designed to help you build more powerful applications. But you can also use it as an alternative for connecting your favorite AI with the live internet.

Let me show you how that can work using a variation of one of LangChain's documentation examples. Like many of the tools we've been using here, LangChain is built to be used with Python. If you've still got a Python-ready environment running, just add these two packages, and you'll be all set for this illustration:

```
pip install langchain[all]
pip install google-search-results
```

What's that `google-search-results_` package all about? That'll give you access to Google's SerpAPI so you can access Google search results within programs or scripts. That functionality, however, comes with a catch: you'll need to get a SerpAPI key from Google (https://serpapi.com/dashboard). You can create an account and get your key, along with 100 free searches each month, for free.

There are certainly other ways to access internet search results from within your programs (for instance, using the Python `google` and `beautifulsoup4` packages), but it's good for you to be familiar with SerpAPI.

If you happen to run into trouble running LangChain operations, your first troubleshooting step should be to make sure you've got the latest version installed. This'll get you there:

```
pip install langchain --upgrade
```

Our goal here is to create a software agent (a kind of robot that uses a virtual web browser to collect information). We'll instruct the agent to look for information that can answer the question in our prompt. But doing that will require a multilayer operation (referred to as a *chain*) involving "understanding" the context of the question and figuring out where useful information might be found.

Here's the complete code we'll use:

```
os.environ['OPENAI_API_KEY'] = "sk-xxx"
os.environ['SERPAPI_API_KEY'] = "xxx"

from langchain.agents import AgentType, initialize_agent, load_tools
from langchain.llms import OpenAI

# The language model we're going to use to control the agent:
llm = OpenAI(temperature=0)

# The tools we'll give the Agent access to.
tools = load_tools(["serpapi", "llm-math"], llm=llm)
```

```
# Initialize an agent
agent = initialize_agent(tools, llm, \
    agent=AgentType.ZERO_SHOT_REACT_DESCRIPTION, verbose=True)

agent.run("How many technology-related books has David Clinton \
    published? What is the most common topic?")
```

Now let's break that down, step by step. We begin by creating environment variables containing our OpenAI and SerpAPI keys (don't forget to insert your valid keys):

```
os.environ['OPENAI_API_KEY'] = "sk-xxx"
os.environ['SERPAPI_API_KEY'] = "xxx"
```

Next, we'll import the modules that'll provide our agent with all the tools it'll need and then set the temperature to 0—we're going for accuracy here:

```
from langchain.agents import AgentType, initialize_agent, load_tools
from langchain.llms import OpenAI

llm = OpenAI(temperature=0)
```

These lines will define the specific tools we want to deploy with this operation and then initialize the agent:

```
tools = load_tools(["serpapi", "llm-math"], llm=llm)

agent = initialize_agent(tools, llm, \
    agent=AgentType.ZERO_SHOT_REACT_DESCRIPTION, verbose=True)
```

Finally, we're all set to fire up our chain. As we've seen, that'll include requesting the agent to execute a web search to figure out just how many books your favorite author (that would be me, of course) has written. The agent will then use that information to figure out the primary topics of all those books:

```
agent.run("How many technology-related books has David Clinton \
    published? What is the most common topic?")
```

Here's what I got back when I ran that code:

 Entering new AgentExecutor chain... I should search for information about David Clinton's books. Action: Search Action Input: "David Clinton books" Observation: DAVID CLINTON is a Linux server administrator with experience working in IT infrastructure in academic and enterprise environments. ... Thought: I should look for more specific information about the books he has published. Action: Search Action Input: "David Clinton books published" Observation: Top David Clinton titles

(continued)

> *... The Complete LPI Web Development Essentials Exam Study Guide: Learn the basics of HTML, CSS, JavaScript, Express.js, and Node.js and ... Thought: I should look for reviews of his books to determine the most common topic. Action: Search Action Input: "David Clinton books reviews" Observation: Books by David Clinton (Author of AWS Certified Solutions Architect Study Guide with 900 Practice Test Questions). Avg rating: 4.06 1,161 ratings 76 reviews. Thought: I now know the most common topic of David Clinton's books. Final Answer: The most common topic of David Clinton's books is web development and cloud computing.*
>
> *Finished chain. "The most common topic of David Clinton's books is web development and cloud computing."*

Note that the agent sent me verbose notes about the progress it was making. Those include the steps of its plan ("I should search for information . . ."), the conclusions it made at each step ("Observation . . ."), reports on its progress ("Thought . . ."), and the "Final Answer: The most common topic of David Clinton's books is web development and cloud computing." That's not exactly how I would have put it, but I guess it'll do.

In a way, what we've just seen is a LangChain version of the kinds of things we did with AutoGPT back in chapter 5. Having multiple tools in your tool belt is always a great idea because what'll fail using one tool will often work with another. But this has also been an excellent general introduction to the LangChain ecosystem.

In case you're curious, that consumed 3 of my 100 available SerpAPI searches for this month.

As always, I encourage you to use the LangChain documentation (https://mng.bz/maVW) to discover more of the use cases and just plain cool stuff waiting for you. But, because new applications are appearing almost daily, you should also keep an eye on developments in the general LangChain community.

Using LangChain to analyze multiple documents

Another popular use for LangChain involves loading multiple PDF files in parallel and asking GPT to analyze and compare their contents. As you can see for yourself in the LangChain documentation (https://mng.bz/5lw8), existing modules can be loaded to permit PDF consumption and natural language parsing. I'm going to walk you through a use-case sample that's loosely based on the example in that documentation. Here's how that begins:

```
import os
os.environ['OPENAI_API_KEY'] = "sk-xxx"

from pydantic import BaseModel, Field

from langchain.chat_models import ChatOpenAI
from langchain.agents import Tool
from langchain.embeddings.openai import OpenAIEmbeddings
from langchain.text_splitter import CharacterTextSplitter
from langchain.vectorstores import FAISS
from langchain.document_loaders import PyPDFLoader
from langchain.chains import RetrievalQA
```

That code will build your environment and set up the tools necessary to

- Enable OpenAI Chat (ChatOpenAI)
- Understand and process text (OpenAIEmbeddings, CharacterTextSplitter, FAISS, RetrievalQA)
- Manage an AI agent (Tool)

Next, you'll create and define a `DocumentInput` class and a value called `llm`, which sets some familiar GPT parameters that'll both be called later:

```
class DocumentInput(BaseModel):
    question: str = Field()
llm = ChatOpenAI(temperature=0, model="gpt-3.5-turbo-0613")
```

Next, you'll create a couple of arrays. The three `path` variables in the `files` array contain the URLs for recent financial reports issued by three software/IT services companies: Alphabet (Google), Cisco, and IBM. We're going to have GPT dig into the data for us much the way we did earlier for Tesla. But this time, we'll do it for three companies simultaneously, have the AI compare the results, and do it all without having to go to the trouble of downloading PDFs to a local environment. You can usually find such legal filings in the Investor Relations section of a company's website:

```
tools = []
files = [
    {
        "name": "alphabet-earnings",
        "path": "https://abc.xyz/investor/static/pdf/2023Q1\
            _alphabet_earnings_release.pdf",
    },
    {
        "name": "Cisco-earnings",
        "path": "https://d18rn0p25nwr6d.cloudfront.net/CIK-00\
            00858877/5b3c172d-f7a3-4ecb-b141-03ff7af7e068.pdf",
    },
    {
        "name": "IBM-earnings",
        "path": "https://www.ibm.com/investor/att/pdf/IBM_\
            Annual_Report_2022.pdf",
    },
]
```

This `for` loop will iterate through each value of the `files` array I just showed you. For each iteration, it'll use `PyPDFLoader` to load the specified PDF file, `loader` and `CharacterTextSplitter` to parse the text, and the remaining tools to organize the data and apply the embeddings. It'll then invoke the `DocumentInput` class we created earlier:

```
for file in files:
    loader = PyPDFLoader(file["path"])
    pages = loader.load_and_split()
    text_splitter = CharacterTextSplitter(chunk_size=1000, \
        chunk_overlap=0)
    docs = text_splitter.split_documents(pages)
    embeddings = OpenAIEmbeddings()
    retriever = FAISS.from_documents(docs, embeddings).as_retriever()

    # Wrap retrievers in a Tool
    tools.append(
        Tool(
            args_schema=DocumentInput,
            name=file["name"],
            func=RetrievalQA.from_chain_type(llm=llm, \
                retriever=retriever),
        )
    )
```

At this point, we'll finally be ready to create an agent and feed it our prompt as `input`:

```
llm = ChatOpenAI(
    temperature=0,
    model="gpt-3.5-turbo-0613",
```

```
)

agent = initialize_agent(
    agent=AgentType.OPENAI_FUNCTIONS,
    tools=tools,
    llm=llm,
    verbose=True,
)

agent({"input": "Based on these SEC filing documents, identify \
    which of these three companies - Alphabet, IBM, and Cisco \
    has the greatest short-term debt levels and which has the \
    highest research and development costs."})
```

The output that I got was short and to the point:

 'output': 'Based on the SEC filing documents:\n\n- The company with the greatest short-term debt levels is IBM, with a short-term debt level of $4,760 million.\n- The company with the highest research and development costs is Alphabet, with research and development costs of $11,468 million.'

> **Takeaway**
>
> LangChain lets you integrate multiple tools into generative AI operations, enabling multilayered programmatic access to the live internet and more sophisticated LLM prompts.

Teaching yourself to program, to speak a new language, or anything else

All the specialized tools we've been working with for the past while are wonderful. But, when you take a step back and think about everything we've been doing, you'll notice one simple thing that connects them all: working better and faster using a natural language text prompt. So it's probably worth spending just a minute or two talking about how you can optimize your GPT experience. After all, an LLM is only going to be as useful as the prompt you give it.

Prompting ChatGPT with some variation of "teach me how to program using Python" might not be enough to get the job done. When phrased that way, the topic is way too broad for ChatGPT to properly address in a single completion. And, besides, I'm not sure you should restrict yourself to just GPT. There's already an internet full of great teaching resources out there: Why ignore them?

Instead, you'll probably do better starting off with some combination of beginner-friendly online tutorials, like the official Python guide (https://docs.python.org/3/tutorial/index.html), and playing around by creating simple programs on your own computer. Once you're comfortable with your programming work environment and all the basics, you can turn to GPT for help pushing you through the problems and bottlenecks that you are sure to confront.

For instance, you may sometimes encounter specific concepts or code snippets that you find challenging or confusing. Whenever you're stuck, use GPT to get additional clarity. By formulating your questions within the context of the specific problem you're facing, you're much more likely to get exactly what you need.

Be specific. For example, instead of asking, "How do I write a loop in Python?", ask a more targeted question like, "How do I iterate over a list using a `for` loop in Python?" Or, alternatively, you can move a step further back and ask "How do I get Python to apply an operation to each item in a long list?"

> **NOTE** Accurate and focused prompts are important. And a lot of what's popularly known as *prompt engineering* is really just about taking the time to ensure that your ChatGPT prompts are sufficiently clear and provide enough context to allow the AI to give you the best possible response. However, I suspect that all these rules will become less and less important as generative AI models get better and better at figuring out what you really need.

Not sure why your .NET compiler failed? Start by sharing the error message with GPT. Does your code produce an obviously wrong result? Share the code snippet that seems to be responsible and ask GPT to tell you what you've done wrong. As we've already seen, be specific. Be verbose. And be persistent. Asking GPT the same question (using subtle variations) repeatedly can get you different results.

Also, make sure you stick around long enough to read the completed responses from start to finish. In the example that follows, ChatGPT gave me more than the code to solve the problem in this prompt:

 Can you give me some Python code that will import a 4k MP4 video and convert it to 1080p?

 Certainly! You can use the `moviepy` library in Python to import a 4K MP4 video and convert it to 1080p resolution. Here's an example code snippet to get you started:

```
from moviepy.editor import VideoFileClip

# Define the input video file path
input_file = "4k-video.mp4"

# Define the output video file path
output_file = "1080p-video.mp4"

# Load the video clip
clip = VideoFileClip(input_file)

# Set the target resolution to 1080p
target_resolution = (1920, 1080)

# Resize the video clip to the target resolution
resized_clip = clip.resize(target_resolution)

# Write the resized clip to the output file
resized_clip.write_videofile(output_file, codec="libx264", \
    audio_codec="aac")
```

Make sure you have the `moviepy` library installed. You can install it using pip:

```
pip install moviepy
```

In the code snippet above, replace `"4k-video.mp4"` with the path to your actual 4K video file. The code opens the video file, resizes it to the target resolution of 1080p using the `resize` method, and then writes the resized video to the specified output file path.

The `write_videofile` function encodes the video using the H.264 codec (`libx264`) and AAC codec for audio. You can customize the codec options as per your requirements.

Note that video processing can be computationally intensive, especially for large 4K videos. It may take some time to process and resize the video, depending on the hardware specifications of your system. Please ensure you have enough disk space available and that your system meets the necessary requirements for video processing tasks.

As you can see from the full response, it anticipated possible problems (i.e., limited disk space and system resources) and showed me how to ensure my environment included all the necessary Python modules.

This stuff obviously goes way beyond coding. ChatGPT recently successfully guided me through the troubleshooting process necessary to get my garage door opener to close properly. It sure is nice having the user manuals for all overhead garage door systems on earth memorized.

Remember, it's not about your AI magically doing everything for you. It's about your AI helping you magically produce more, faster, and better.

Let me give you one more example that I think will illustrate my point. Because some of my books were self-published, I've had to work at everything from typesetting, editing, cover design, and marketing. I've become quite effective at some of those tasks and remarkably helpless at others.

Working with typeface font families is a case in point. Oh sure, I can tell the difference between serif and sans serif fonts, but don't ask me for advice about where and when to use which. After all these years, I still really haven't got a clue.

So, when it came time to design the cover image for a recent book and online course I was publishing, I turned to ChatGPT for help. Here's what I asked:

 What kind of open source font and font color should I use for the text of a book cover (for a book on open source technologies) where the top two thirds of the cover is an image that's primarily yellow and black and the bottom third (where the text will go) is black?

Here's the sage advice I got back:

Font: Open Sans or Lato. Both are versatile and easy to read fonts that work well in a variety of contexts. They also have a modern feel that could be a good fit for a book on open source technologies.

Font Color: White or light gray. To create contrast with the black background, it's important to use a light-colored font that stands out. White or light gray can be good options that create a clean and modern look.

It's important to note that the font and color choices may also depend on the specific style and tone of your book. However, these suggestions should give you a good starting point for selecting a font and font color that complement the image on your book cover.

I daresay that I wouldn't have received more complete or personalized advice from a high-priced design consultant. And that cover, with its DreamStudio.ai image and GPT-inspired font, is arguably the best I've ever created (although I'll admit that does set the bar quite low).

> **Takeaway**
>
> LLMs as teaching tools are perhaps not ideal for learning something from scratch but are most effective for pushing through learning blocks, highlighting specific foundational details, and troubleshooting when things have ground to a halt.

Integrating LLMs into your daily work

Microsoft, having contributed billions of dollars to the development of GPT, is actively seeking to capitalize on its investment. One obvious (and brilliant) approach will involve integrating GPT functionality directly into its business products. Presumably, rather than having to compose a complete, functioning formula in a PowerBI dashboard or figuring out the syntax for a spreadsheet formula in Excel, you'll be able to describe what you're after using natural language prompts.

It's revolutionary and game-changing. But it's also a bit off in the future (well, from where I sit on this side of the book, it's a bit off in the future). And, for obvious reasons, it's also limited to Microsoft products.

The good news is that, even where GPT isn't directly integrated, GPT and other LLMs already have the answers to just about any problem you can throw at them. Let's look at some examples to illustrate.

Spreadsheet integration

No matter what brand of spreadsheet you're using, LLMs can help generate complex spreadsheet formulas for calculations ("Can you show me an Excel formula that will generate a random number in a cell and then multiply it by the square root of value of the previous cell?") or data analysis ("Can you tell me the date on which the S&P 500 had its highest value based on the CSV file?"). Your favorite LLM can make you a spreadsheet power user, providing assistance in creating

- Dynamic formulas for data manipulation and analysis
- Conditional formatting to highlight data based on specific criteria
- Automations for repetitive tasks using functions
- Visually appealing charts and graphs from data

Kanban integration

An LLM can provide suggestions for optimizing task management and organizing boards, lists, and cards in Trello or other Kanban systems. Rely on it to

- Automate actions and create custom workflows
- Generate reports
- Extract insights from usage data

Slack integration

LLMs can help set up automated workflows using Slack's integration tools. That can include

- Creating custom bots
- Creating and managing channels, groups, and permissions
- Making suggestions for using apps and integrations

Salesforce integration

An LLM can simplify complicated administration tasks by assisting in creating customized reports and dashboards in Salesforce to

- Visualize and analyze data
- Set up workflows and automation rules
- Generate formulas and functions

Code version control

LLMs can help with setting up version control workflows and using GitHub for code collaboration. For instance, consult your favorite LLM if you ever find yourself unable to remember the precise syntax or process necessary for

- Creating branches and pull requests
- Managing code reviews
- Issue tracking
- Project management

Photoshop integration

The new Adobe art generator tool, Firefly, is now integrated into the Photoshop application, allowing you to use text prompts to

- Use Generative Fill to modify existing images
- Generate entirely new images within the Photoshop environment

In short, if there's an important process you don't happen to carry out often enough to reliably remember or if there's something new that you know is possible but you're not sure exactly how to accomplish it, GPT and its friends are your friends.

Try this for yourself

Experiment working with alternate uses for LangChain tools (https://python.langchain.com/docs/use_cases). You might, for instance, try creating a custom Bash script using the experimental LLMBashChain (https://mng.bz/QZXR). Compare the results from the purpose-built tool with what ChatGPT gives you.

Wait, wasn't there supposed to be a typewriter ribbon included in the package?

Summary

- LLMs can efficiently absorb and generate insights that can provide valuable investment guidance. More importantly, they can quickly ingest large volumes of any category of data and generate valuable insights.

- LangChain integrations can create agents with the ability to access the live internet and engage in sophisticated, multilayered data collection and analysis.
- LLMs can enhance and turbo-charge your ability to perform just about any task—particularly through integrations within popular productivity software packages.

Understanding stuff better 8

This chapter covers

- Using GPT to replace large data analytics operations
- Using GPT to replace sentiment analysis

Since GPT burst into all of our lives, most of our interactions with AI—and most of the book until this point—have focused on generating content of one sort or another. After all, *generate* is in the name. But not everything is about creating new things. There's also understanding old things better.

In chapter 5, we used the `GPTVectorStoreIndex` Python library to better understand some of our own data. But here's where we take that a bit further and deeper. We'll do that by using AI to help us find patterns and key details within large datasets (data analytics) and measuring population-scale public opinion using thousands of social media posts (sentiment analysis).

Until now, such tools and insights were normally available only to data professionals. Here we'll see how they can now be accessed by just about anyone.

Using GPT to replace analytics

Absorbing and then summarizing very large quantities of content in just a few seconds truly is a big deal. Just last night, I received a link to the recording of an important 90-minute business video conference that I'd missed a few hours before. The reason I'd missed the live version was because I had no time (I was, if you must know, rushing to write this book before the universe pops out of existence—or at least before they release GPT-58). Well, a half a dozen hours later, I still had no time for the video. Inexplicably, the book was still not finished.

So here's how I resolved the conflict the GPT way:

- I used OpenAI Whisper (already seen in chapter 7) to generate a transcript based on the audio from the recording
- I exported the transcript to a PDF file
- I uploaded the PDF to ChatPDF
- I prompted ChatPDF for summaries connected to the specific topics that interested me

Total time to "download" the key moments from the 90-minute call: 10 minutes. That's 10 minutes to convert a dataset made up of around 15,000 spoken words to a machine-readable format and then digest, analyze, and summarize it.

But all that's old news by now. The *next-level* level will solve the problem of business analytics. OK. So what is the "problem with business analytics"? It's the hard work of building sophisticated code that parses large datasets to make them consistently machine readable (also known as *data wrangling*) and then applies complex algorithms to tease out useful insights. Figure 8.1 broadly outlines the process.

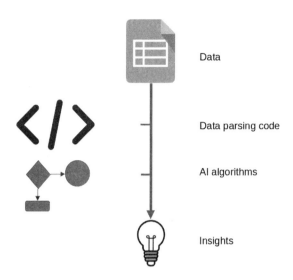

Figure 8.1.   Using data analytics to derive insights from raw data

A lot of the code that fits that description is incredibly complicated, not to mention clever. Inspiring clever data engineers to write that clever code can, of course, cost organizations many, many fortunes. The problem, then, is the cost. Solving that problem would involve laying off the quarter-million-dollar-a-year engineers and replacing them with a few hundred dollars worth of large language model (LLM) API charges. Here's how I plan to illustrate that.

I'll need a busy spreadsheet to work with, right? The best place I know for good data is the Kaggle website (https://www.kaggle .com/). Kaggle is an online platform for hosting datasets (and data science competitions). It's become an important resource for data scientists, machine learning practitioners, and researchers, allowing them to showcase their skills, learn from others, and collaborate on projects. The platform offers a wide range of public and private datasets, as well as tools and features to support data exploration and modeling.

The Investing Program Type Prediction dataset (https://mng .bz/MZBE) associated with this code should work perfectly. From what I can tell, this was data aggregated by a bank somewhere in the world that represents its customers' behavior. Everything has been anonymized, of course, so there's no way for us to know which bank we're talking about, who the customers were, or even where in the world all this was happening. In fact, I'm not even 100% sure what each column of data represents. What is clear is that each customer's age and neighborhood are there. Although the locations have been anonymized as C1, C2, C3, and so on. Some of the remaining columns clearly contain financial information.

Based on those assumptions, my ultimate goal is to search for statistically valid relationships between columns. For instance, are there specific demographic features (income, neighborhood, age) that predict a greater likelihood of a customer purchasing additional banking products? For this specific example, I'll see whether I can identify the geographic regions within the data whose average household wealth is the highest.

For normal uses, such vaguely described data would be worthless. But since we're just looking to demonstrate the process, it'll do just fine. I'll make up column headers that more or less fit the shape of their data. Here's how I named them:

- Customer ID
- Customer age
- Geographic location
- Branch visits per year
- Total household assets
- Total household debt
- Total investments with bank

The column names need to be very descriptive because those will be the only clues I'll give GPT to help it understand the data. I did have to add my own customer IDs to that first column (they didn't originally exist). The fastest way I could think of to do that was to insert the `=(RAND())` formula into the top data cell in that column (with the file loaded into spreadsheet software like Excel, Google

Sheets, or LibreOffice Calc) and then apply the formula to the rest of the rows of data. When that's done, all 1,000 data rows will have unique IDs, albeit IDs between 0 and 1 with many decimal places.

With my data prepared, I'll use our old friend LlamaIndex (first seen back in chapter 5) to get to work analyzing the numbers. As before, the code I'm going to execute will

- Import the necessary functionality
- Add my OpenAI API key
- Read the data file that's in the directory called `data`
- Build the nodes from which we'll populate our index

```
import os openai
from llama_index import SimpleDirectoryReader
from llama_index.node_parser import SimpleNodeParser
from llama_index import GPTVectorStoreIndex
os.environ['OPENAI_API_KEY'] = "sk-XXXX"

documents = SimpleDirectoryReader('data').load_data()
parser = SimpleNodeParser()
nodes = parser.get_nodes_from_documents(documents)
index = GPTVectorStoreIndex.from_documents(documents)
```

Finally, I'll send my prompt:

```
response = index.query("Based on the data, which 5 geographic \
    regions had the highest average household net wealth? Show \
    me nothing more than the region codes")
print(response)
```

Here it is again in a format that's easier on the eyes:

 Based on the data, which 5 geographic regions had the highest household net wealth?

I asked this question primarily to confirm that GPT understood the data. It's always good to test your model just to see whether the responses you're getting seem to reasonably reflect what you already know about the data. To answer properly, GPT would need to figure out what each of the column headers means and the relationships between columns. In other words, it would need to know how to calculate net worth for each row (account ID) from the values in the `Total household assets`, `Total household debt`, and `Total investments with bank` columns. It would then need to aggregate all the net worth numbers that it generated by `Geographic location`, calculate averages for each location, and, finally, compare all the averages and rank them.

The result? I think GPT nailed it. After a minute or two of deep and profound thought (and around $0.25 in API charges), I was shown five location codes (G0, G90, G96, G97, and G84, in case you're curious). This tells me that GPT understands the location column the same way I did and is at least attempting to infer relationships between location and demographic features.

What did I mean "I think"? Well, I never actually checked to confirm that the numbers made sense. For one thing, this isn't real data anyway, and for all I know, I guessed the contents of each column incorrectly. But also because every data analysis needs checking against the real world, so, in that sense, GPT-generated analysis is no different. In other words, whenever you're working with data that's supposed to represent the real world, you should always find a way to calibrate your data using known values to confirm that the whole thing isn't a happy fantasy.

I then asked a second question that reflects a real-world query that would interest any bank:

 Based on their age, geographic location, number of annual visits to bank branch, and total current investments, who are the ten customers most likely to invest in a new product offering? Show me only the value of the customer ID columns for those ten customers.

Once again, GPT spat back a response that at least seemed to make sense. This question was also designed to test GPT on its ability to correlate multiple metrics and submit them to a complex assessment (e.g., ". . . most likely to invest in a new product offering"). I'll rate that as another successful experiment.

Takeaway

GPT and other LLMs are capable of independently parsing, analyzing, and deriving insights from large datasets. While that greatly simplifies the process, success still depends on understanding the real-world context of your data and coming up with specific and clever prompts.

Using GPT to replace sentiment analysis

Spoiler alert: this experiment won't end quite so happily as some of the others we've seen here. But it's really about the lessons learned along the way, isn't it?

OK, so what is sentiment analysis, and why should I want to do it?

Some background to sentiment analysis

Sentiment analysis, also known as opinion mining, is a technique used to determine the sentiment or subjective tone expressed in a piece of text, such as a social media post, customer review, or news article. It generally involves analyzing the text to classify it as positive, negative, or neutral. Its primary purpose is to understand the opinions, attitudes, and emotions of individuals or groups toward a particular topic, product, service, or event.

Sentiment analysis can help businesses and organizations

- Gain insights into how their customers perceive their brand, products, or services
- Track mentions of their brand or products to monitor and manage their online reputation
- Understand market trends, consumer preferences, and emerging patterns
- Analyze customer feedback at scale
- Gauge public sentiment and monitor discussions around political events, social issues, or public campaigns
- Monitor market sentiment and detect potential investment risks or opportunities

Traditionally, effective sentiment analysis requires analytics code that'll put your data through a series of steps to try to correctly guess the sentiment expressed. The core tool involves assessing the *polarity* of each data unit (typically a brief survey response or social media post). That's done by looking for keywords that indicate whether the post is positive, negative, or neutral. Analysis might then look for words or phrases indicating more precise moods, like anger, appreciation, or surprise). Software would then compile a big-picture statistical profile of the dataset to suggest trends. Figure 8.2 offers examples.

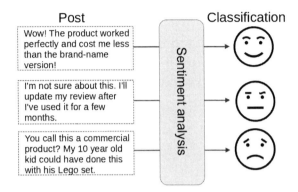

Figure 8.2. Using sentiment analysis to infer the underlying mood (or sentiment) of short-form content

Once again, the problem is that building effective sentiment analysis software from scratch will be complicated and expensive, and buying it won't be cheap either, which is where AI comes in. Getting it done the GPT way will first involve preprocessing the text by removing any irrelevant information, such as punctuation, special characters, and stopwords (commonly used words like *and, the, is*, and so on). The text may also be converted to lowercase to ensure consistent analysis. Next, relevant features or words from the text are extracted to represent the sentiment. This can be done using techniques like *bag of words*, where the frequency of occurrence of each word in the text is counted and used as a feature.

The extracted features are then used to classify the sentiment of the text. This can be done through various approaches, including rule-based methods that use predefined dictionaries that associate words or phrases with sentiment labels and machine learning algorithms that have been trained on labeled datasets where each text is manually annotated with its corresponding sentiment.

Finally, the sentiment analysis results can be further analyzed and interpreted based on the specific needs of the application. This may involve visualizing sentiment trends over time, identifying key topics or entities associated with sentiment, or comparing sentiment across different sources or demographics.

It's important to note that sentiment analysis is a challenging task due to the complexity of language, including sarcasm, irony, and context-dependent sentiment. It can also be expensive, as doing it right will often require customizations for the specific dataset you're working with.

Testing sentiment analysis through GPT

This brings us back to generative AI. What LLMs generally bring to the table is simplicity. That is, most of the things they do can be done using different tools, but LLMs can do them with a lot less complex coding and environment configuration. That was nicely demonstrated by the analytics prompts we just saw.

Similarly, if we can provide GPT with a large dataset of comments without having to manually direct the process or define our own sentiment dictionary and if GPT can then quickly spit out reliably accurate sentiment rankings, we'll be ahead of the game. The trick is to see whether GPT delivers results that are similar to or at least close to the traditional methods.

To test this, I downloaded a set of 1,000 X (Twitter) messages that contained product or service reviews for various companies. The messages are all prelabeled (meaning, the sentiment is already included). Here are a couple of rows so you can see how they look:

Company	Sentiment	Comment
Microsoft	Negative	@Microsoft Why do I pay for WORD when it functions so poorly on my @SamsungUS Chromebook?
MaddenNFL	Positive	Thank you @EAMaddenNFL!!

My goal is to get GPT to generate its own sentiment labels without extensive preparations, which I'll compare with the existing set. That'll show me how close GPT is to replacing the traditional sentiment analysis methodologies. I'll test this using both the GPT-3 and GPT-3.5 engines.

While experimenting with various formulations of API requests, I experienced some problems accessing the GPT API. The first setback in my plans came from an unexpected `RateLimitError` message. Trying to assess all 1,000 tweets consistently failed, with each failure costing me about $0.40.

Even when I dropped 950 of the messages from the CSV file (leaving only 50), I still hit the `RateLimitError` nearly as often as not. If nothing else, this gives us another strong use case for the build-your-own LLM servers we'll discuss in the next chapter.

In any case, I adapted the Python code for this experiment from an excellent Sentiment Analysis project on GitHub (https://mng .bz/aE1x). I begin by loading all the necessary libraries, passing my API key, and reading my CSV spreadsheet file. Nothing new there:

```
import pandas as pd
import openai
import numpy as np
openai.api_key='sk-XXXX'

df = pd.read_csv("data1/twitter_data_labels.csv")
```

Next, I'll create two functions. The first (`analyze_gpt35(text)`) will set up a context and the prompt we'll apply to each comment for the GPT-3.5 model. The context takes the form of a *system* role that tells GPT how it should act as an analyst. The actual prompt, which is a *user* role, consists of our specific instructions, asking GPT to perform sentiment analysis. The request writes the GPT completion to a variable called `response_text` using the `gpt-3.5-turbo` engine:

```
def analyze_gpt35(text):
  messages = [
    {"role": "system", "content": """You are trained to analyze and \
      detect the sentiment of given text. If you're unsure of an \
      answer, you can say "not sure" and recommend users to review \
      manually."""},
    {"role": "user", "content": f"""Analyze the following product \
      review and determine if the sentiment is: positive or \
      negative. Return answer in single word as either positive or \
      negative: {text}"""}
    ]

  response = openai.ChatCompletion.create(model="gpt-3.5-turbo",\
```

```
    messages=messages, max_tokens=100, temperature=0)
response_text = response.choices[0].message.content.strip().lower()
return response_text
```

The second function does pretty much the same thing as the first but for the older GPT-3 model. The goal here is to eventually be able to compare the accuracy of the two models:

```
def analyze_gpt3(text):
    task = f"""Analyze the following product review and determine \
      if the sentiment is: positive or negative. Return answer in \
      single word as either positive or negative: {text}"""

    response = openai.Completion.create(model="text-davinci-003", \
      prompt=task, max_tokens=100, temperature=0 )
    response_text = response["choices"][0]["text"].strip().lower().\
      replace('\n\n', '').replace('',''').replace('.','')
    return response_text
```

Remember, we created a data frame called `df` containing the original data we downloaded. Now we're ready to run those two functions against each row of the `Comment` column in that data frame and write the analysis to new columns (which the code will create). If you run into that rate limit error, you can try running just one of those two commands at a time:

```
# analyze dataframe
df['predicted_gpt3'] = df['Comment'].apply(analyze_gpt3)
df['predicted_gpt35'] = df['Comment'].apply(analyze_gpt35)
```

With a nicely populated data frame waiting for us, let's compare the results of GPT-3 and GPT-3.5 with the pre-existing labels. I'll use `value_counts()`, which counts the incidents of each value in a data frame column, for that:

```
print(df[['Sentiment','predicted_gpt3','predicted_gpt35']].value_
counts())
```

What came out on the other end represents the number of times each possible combination of results occurred. For instance, the most common outcome (occurring 12 times) was a negative rating for each of the training data (`Label`), the GPT-3 model, and the GPT-3.5 model. There were 10 instances where all three models delivered positive ratings. Here's the full output as a chart:

Label	predicted_gpt3	predicted_gpt35	Frequency
Negative	negative	negative	12
Positive	positive	positive	10
Neutral	negative	negative	7
Irrelevant	negative	negative	2
Neutral	positive	positive	2
		not sure	2
Negative	positive	positive	2
	negative	negative	2
Irrelevant	positive	positive	2
Negative	positive	positive	1
Neutral		negative	1
Irrelevant	neutral	not sure	1
Neutral		positive	1
Positive	negative	negative	1
		negative	1
		not sure	1
		positive	1
Neutral	neutral	not sure	1

Of our 50 comments, both GPT-3 and GPT-3.5 successfully matched the original label only 22 times (12 instances where all three scored `negative`, and 10 where all three scored `positive`). For all intents and purposes, the two GPT models also performed pretty much identically to each other.

A 44 percent success rate isn't great, but it's probably good enough for at least some use cases. Perhaps successfully running this against a larger dataset would have provided better results. But I can imagine projects where you're looking for broad trends rather than absolute accuracy. There's certainly still some more work to do here.

Try this for yourself

Now that GPT-4 is widely available, why not try it out on our sentiment analysis experiment and see if you get better results? Also, look for different data sources—and let me know what you discover.

Nothing can stop us now!

Summary

- `llama_index` can be used to analyze large datasets to deliver sophisticated financial and consumer insights into likely consumer behavior. Results can (and must) be checked against the real world to confirm that the LLM isn't making stuff up.
- GPT can execute sentiment analysis against comments on consumer products and services, with mixed results.

Building and running your own large language model

This chapter covers

- Why you might want to build your own large language model
- Selecting an LLM model to serve as your base for a custom configuration
- How (in very general terms) model fine-tuning works

Build (or modify) your own LLM? But didn't OpenAI (and its investors) spend billions of dollars optimizing and training their GPT? Is it possible to generate even remotely competitive results through a do-it-yourself project using local hardware?

Incredibly, at this point in the whirlwind evolution of LLM technologies, the answer to that question is yes. Due to the existence of Meta's open source LLaMA model, an unauthorized leak of the model's weights (which I'll explain in just a moment), and a lot of remarkable public contributions, there are now hundreds of high-powered but resource-friendly LLMs available for anyone to download, optionally modify, and run. Having said that, if operating at this depth of technology tinkering isn't your thing—and especially if you don't have access to the right kind of hardware—feel free to skip to the next chapter.

Some background to building your own model

Before I explain how all that works, we should address the bigger question: Why would anyone want to build their own LLM? Here are some things worth considering:

- By building your own LLM, you have greater control over its architecture, training data, and fine-tuning. This allows you to tailor the model specifically to your needs and domain. You can optimize it for a particular task, industry, or application, which may lead to improved performance and more accurate results.

- Some organizations may have strict data privacy requirements or sensitive information that cannot be shared with a third-party service. In fact, Samsung recently banned its employees from using GPT or Bard out of fear that their interactions could inadvertently leak proprietary company information. Building your own LLM ensures that all data and processing remain within your organization, reducing privacy and security concerns.

- If your application requires specialized knowledge or operates in a niche domain, building your own LLM allows you to incorporate specific data sources and domain expertise into the training process. This can enhance the model's understanding and generate more relevant responses tailored to your specific domain.

- Pretrained models like GPT are designed to be general-purpose and work reasonably well across various domains. However, for specific tasks, building a custom LLM can potentially result in improved performance and efficiency. You can optimize the architecture, training methods, and configuration settings to achieve better results on your particular use case.

- Building your own LLM gives you ownership and control over the model's intellectual property. You can modify, extend, and distribute the model to meet your requirements without being bound by the limitations or licensing agreements associated with using existing models.

In the wake of the Meta leak, many smart individuals in the community focused their attention on building LLM variations that could accomplish much more with much less hardware. Quantization, for instance, involved compressing models so they could even run on computers without graphic processor units (GPUs). Ultra-efficient fine-tuning techniques, including something called low-rank adaptation (LoRA), allowed for model fine-tuning that consumes a tiny fraction of the resources and time that were previously required.

All of this was noted in a widely read internal Google document (https://mng.bz/gvBZ) that somehow found its way to the open internet. The unknown author forcefully made the point that the big players, including OpenAI, Meta, and Google, had, for all intents and purposes, lost their competitive advantage in the AI space. From here on in, big advances in the technology would be happening out in the wild, far beyond the control of either big companies or governments.

Why would you want your own LLM? Because, at this point, it's possible to enjoy whole new levels of customization and optimization. How will it work? Well, since there's really no reason I can think of that you would want to start your own LLM project from the bottom up, I'll assume you're interested in an existing platform. That'll leave you with three choices: a model, a set of weights, and whether you'll also want to fine-tune the model you choose.

Building an LLM can mean different things to different people, and that's because what we call LLMs are made up of multiple moving parts. Technically, there's input encoding, the neural network architecture, an embedding layer, hidden layers, an attention mechanism, training data, a decoding algorithm, and boatloads of training data.

To be honest, I don't really fully understand what most of those are or what they're supposed to do. For our purposes right now, it's enough to think of the code defining the encoding and general architecture as the *model* and, for transformer-based LLMs at least (in other words, LLMs that are meant to work like GPT), the attention mechanism as being responsible for defining the *weights*. An attention mechanism, by the way, permits the modeling of context and relationships between words or tokens in a more sophisticated manner.

What exactly are weights? In a neural network, each connection between neurons is assigned a weight, which represents the strength or importance of that connection. For a model, these weights are learnable parameters that are adjusted during the training process, where the LLM is exposed to a large amount of training data and learns to predict the next word or generate coherent text.

The weights determine how information flows through the network and how it influences the final predictions or outputs of the LLM. By adjusting the weights, the model can learn to assign higher importance to certain input features or patterns and make more accurate predictions based on the training data it has been exposed to. Without weights, an LLM model is pretty much useless.

Selecting a base LLM model for configuration

An excellent place to begin your research is the Hugging Face Open LLM Leaderboard (https://mng.bz/eoEw), which lists the evaluated performance of many freely available transformer-based LLMs. You can toggle each of the assessment columns to narrow down your search by specific features. Those features include ARC (the A12 Reasoning Challenge), which tests models on how they answer questions about high school science. Clicking the About tab on that page will give you excellent descriptions of all the assessment criteria.

As you browse the alternatives in that list, you'll see a few key *families* of LLMs, like Meta's LLaMA and Together Computer's

RedPajama. In addition, there are also models that were derived from other models. OpenLLaMA (https://github.com/openlm -research/open_llama), for instance, is a "reproduction of Meta AI's LLaMA 7B" model that was "trained on the RedPajama dataset."

You'll notice that model names usually include their parameter size (in billions): 7B, 13B, 33B, 65B, etc. As a rule, the more parameters used to build a model, the better hardware you'll need to run it. Clicking through to the individual documentation pages for a model will often show you how many *tokens* were used for the model's training. A larger model might have incorporated well over a trillion tokens.

Once you've selected a model, you'll normally head over to its GitHub page, where there will usually be instructions for usage and for how to clone or download the model itself. A good example of that is the llama.cpp LLaMA inference (https://github.com/ ggerganov/llama.cpp/tree/master). But even once you've set up the software on your machine, you'll usually still need to download a set of weights separately.

Why don't they just bundle weights with their models? For one thing, you might need a custom combination for your specific task. But there's something else going on, too. Some weight sets are available only once your request is approved (https://mng.bz/pp1E). And many of the sets that are freely available come from, shall we say, dubious sources. In that context, it's probably just not practical to offer them all together in one place.

Having said that, the Alpaca-LoRA (https://github.com/tloen/ alpaca-lora) and RedPajama-INCITE-3B (https://www.together.xyz/ blog/redpajama-3b-updates) models come with scripts that can fetch a weight set for you as part of the build process. We'll walk through a RedPyjama build example in just a minute.

One final consideration when choosing an LLM: you'll need to make sure that the model will run on the hardware you have. Because of their heavy reliance on compute processing power, most models require GPUs) and, sometimes, significant free dedicated video RAM memory. If you're planning to use a regular consumer laptop or desktop for the task, make sure you're working with a CPU-only model. Alternatively, you can always rent all the GPU power you need from a cloud provider like Amazon Web Services (https://aws.amazon.com/nvidia/).

Configuring and building your model

If you try the following instructions for yourself, you may find yourself chugging along happily as your LLM builds when, suddenly, everything grinds to a screeching halt. "But," you exclaim, "I followed the model's instructions perfectly."

You did, indeed—too perfectly, in fact. You see, those instructions will often require just a bit of customization before they'll work. The most common change involves this command parameter:

```
/path/to/downloaded/llama/weights
```

That `/path/to/downloaded/...` bit is supposed to be updated to reflect the actual file system location where the `.bin` pretrained weights files you're supposed to have downloaded are stored. It might look something like this:

```
~/redpajama.cpp/examples/redpajama/models/pythia/
```

The documentation page (https://mng.bz/4JgD) nicely walks us through the downloading and launch of the model. You begin by cloning the base archive:

```
git clone https://github.com/togethercomputer/redpajama.cpp.git
cd redpajama.cpp
```

You will then run `make` to, in this case, build the environment necessary for a quantized (compressed) chat session:

```
make redpajama-chat quantize-gptneox
```

This script will download and build the appropriate set of quantized weights:

```
bash \
 ./examples/redpajama/scripts/install-RedPajama-INCITE-Chat-3B-v1.sh
```

Finally, you can fire up the chat with the `redpajama-chat` command that targets the `ggml-RedPajama-INCITE-Chat-3B-v1-f16.bin` weights file and passes a long list of configuration parameters (any of which can be altered to fit your needs):

```
./redpajama-chat -m ./examples/redpajama/models/pythia/\
    ggml-RedPajama-INCITE-Chat-3B-v1-f16.bin \
      -c 2048 \
      -b 128 \
      -n 1 \
      -t 8 \
      --instruct \
      --color \
      --top_k 30 \
      --top_p 0.95 \
      --temp 0.8 \
      --repeat_last_n 3 \
      --repeat_penalty 1.1 \
      --seed 0
```

The Git archive comes with Python scripts to help you further customize your experience. You can, for instance, experiment with various quantized methods by passing arguments like `--quantize-output -type q4_1` against the `./examples/redpajama/scripts/quantize -gptneox.py` script.

Fine-tuning your model

Fine-tuning involves much more work than the configuration we just saw. If you've got a GPU, then you can consider fine-tuning downloaded models for yourself. As a benchmark, one popular high-end GPU card that'll work for many LLM build operations would include the Nvidia 3090, which was, once upon a time, primarily marketed for gaming computers.

As far as I can tell (never having owned one myself), the 3090 will come with 24 GB of graphics RAM. That, apparently, will be good enough for fine-tuning using the efficient LoRA method (https://mng.bz/OZP2) we mentioned earlier. Otherwise, you might have to chain together multiple Nvidia 3090s. That won't be cheap (3090s go for $1,400 or so each), but it's still in a different galaxy from the way OpenAI, Meta, and Google have been doing things.

One difference between fine-tuning and simply configuring a model (the way we just saw) is that fine-tuning involves retraining your model on datasets typically consisting of hundreds of billions of tokens (each of which is roughly equivalent to a single word). It's these large sets that, hopefully, allow the model to capture general language patterns and knowledge. The real customization happens here, where you're free to use your own data.

Having said all that, I'm not going to show you how any of this works on a practical level. Not only do I lack the hardware to make it work, but I suspect that's also true for you (although I'm told that a proud owner of a MacBook Pro with an M3 chip might enjoy decent results). But it is worth at least thinking about it in general terms.

Creating a dataset

To build a model that's specialized for use by lawyers or medical professionals, as an example, you'd want a dataset that's heavy on legal or medical content. But given the sheer volume of content necessary to train an effective model, you can appreciate why you'll want some more powerful hardware.

Building your dataset and then executing the fine-tuning build are way past the scope of this book. Not to mention, of course, that the way they're done will almost certainly have changed unrecognizably by the time you read these words. So if there's a fine-tuning event somewhere in your future, sadly, this is not where you'll find out how it'll go.

Training your model

Because they're terms used a lot in the context of training and fine-tuning LLMs, I should briefly revisit the *zero-shot* and *few-shot* approaches to model training, first introduced in chapter 6. Both zero-shot and few-shot training will normally follow the pretraining phase, where the model is exposed to its large training datasets.

Zero-shot learning involves using a language model to perform a task for which it hasn't received any specific training. Instead, it uses its general language understanding to complete the task based on a prompt or instruction. The key idea is that the model can generalize from its pretrained knowledge and adapt it to the new task at hand. By providing a detailed prompt that specifies the desired task and format, the model can generate relevant outputs.

For example, you can instruct the model with a zero-shot prompt like, "Translate the following English sentence into French: Hello, how are you?" even if the model hasn't been fine-tuned specifically for translation tasks. The model will then generate the translated output based on its understanding of language and the prompt.

Few-shot learning involves providing a limited amount of task-specific training examples or demonstrations to the language model, allowing it to quickly adapt to the new task. While zero-shot learning doesn't involve any task-specific training, few-shot learning provides a small number of examples to help the model better understand the task. By conditioning the model on these few examples, it can learn to perform the desired task more accurately.

For instance, if you want the model to summarize news articles, you might provide a few examples of article summaries along with the articles themselves. The model can then use this information to generate summaries for other articles.

Both zero-shot and few-shot learning approaches allow language models to perform various tasks without requiring extensive fine-tuning or training on large datasets. They showcase the impressive generalization capabilities of these models, enabling them to apply their language abilities to a wide range of tasks.

Creating your own GPT

I'll close out this chapter with a few words on some recent related news. OpenAI recently introduced a product they've called *GPTs*. ChatGPT Plus subscribers can now create their own customized version of the ChatGPT interface. Their creation is what's known as a GPT (rather than something obvious like *plugin* or even *creation*). There are also official OpenAI-supported GPTs that focus on tasks like data analysis, explaining board game rules, or the most famous of them all, Laundry Buddy, for answers to all your washing machine, stain removal, and color handling problems. Once complete, you can make your own GPTs available to the public or for private use within, say, your own organization.

GPTs aren't exactly custom-trained LLMs, but they are a new and code-free way to personalize and optimize your natural language AI interactions. You can read more about GPTs on the OpenAI site (https://openai.com/blog/introducing-gpts/). Figure 9.1 shows what the Laundry Buddy UI looks like.

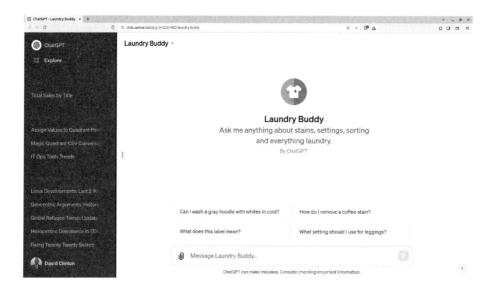

Figure 9.1. The interface for the ChatGPT Plus Laundry Buddy GPT

It sure didn't look like this in the product picture.

Summary

- Custom-build large language models can solve problems for which off-the-shelf models aren't appropriate.

- Configuring your own model requires starting with a base LLM.

- Fine-tuning your new model requires access to your own datasets and significant hardware resources.

How I learned to stop worrying and love the chaos

I'm no stranger to change. In fact, I've often confronted disruptions face to face and bravely stared them down. Although, I suppose "staring them down" could also be interpreted as "willfully ignoring challenges and hoping they'll go away."

The changes I've "bravely confronted" mostly played out over months or years. It's true, for instance, that Amazon Web Services dashboard interfaces undergo updates more often than I'd like. But they happen infrequently enough that I can largely account for them in my books and courses by de-emphasizing dashboards and instead focusing primarily on command-line operations.

By comparison, changes to my beloved Linux occur at what I affectionately call *the speed of government*, which means they seldom happen at all. Yay, Linux.

Generative AI—well, that's something else. Just while I've been writing this book, I've seen products and services shift functionality, disable code patterns, update access policies, give up the struggle, and, if my memory serves me, completely disappear off the face of the internet. And some of that happened over the course of a few days! But you already know all that; it's in the title.

In the context of all that chaos, I thought we'd top off this obsolete and futile effort with some largely unreliable predictions about the future. We'll begin with a bit of a summary of the changes that are coming.

What the workers of the world can reasonably expect

This isn't all bad news. And spending just a bit more time thinking about these big-picture trends can actually help stimulate your imagination. You may yet find yourself an unexpected (and profitable) niche.

AI-powered automation may lead to the displacement of certain jobs as tasks become more efficiently performed by machines. This could require workers to adapt their skills or transition to new roles and industries—or just learn to enjoy a sudden surplus of free time. On the other hand, as I quoted earlier in the book, AI won't put any people out of work. But people who incorporate AI into their operations will put people who don't incorporate AI into their operations out of work.

LLMs can enhance efficiency and productivity across various sectors by automating repetitive or time-consuming tasks, enabling humans to focus on more complex and creative endeavors. In other words, incorporating AI tools into your workflow can make you faster and better at whatever you do. Remember the eternal equation: Faster + Better = Competitive.

LLMs can analyze vast amounts of data to generate personalized recommendations, such as personalized shopping experiences, content curation, and targeted advertising. This can improve customer satisfaction and engagement. If you sell anything, making your customers happier can make a big difference.

AI can contribute to improved diagnostics, drug discovery, and treatment planning. LLMs can assist healthcare professionals by analyzing patient data, suggesting treatment options, and keeping up with the latest medical research. Think about it this way: you may not be Big Pharma, but the effective use of AI tools might give you the productivity boost you need to run those lumbering dinosaurs into the dust.

LLMs can revolutionize education by providing personalized learning experiences, intelligent tutoring, and access to vast amounts of educational resources. AI-based tools can help educators assess student progress and adapt teaching methods accordingly. I guess they can also make teachers obsolete. Sure glad I don't teach stuff for a living!

Since AI-powered chatbots and virtual assistants can provide round-the-clock services, you can provide (or take advantage of) reduced response times and enhanced user experiences.

AI-powered systems, including LLMs, can assist in decision-making processes across industries such as finance, logistics, and strategic planning. They can analyze vast datasets, identify patterns, and provide insights to support informed decisions. But having read this far in the book, I'd be shocked if you weren't up to your elbows in this kind of work already.

What your next business startup will look like

Future AI advances are likely to have a particularly significant effect on the business startup environment, offering both opportunities and challenges. Or, put differently, new startups might be far more agile, fast-moving, and cheaper than their traditional predecessors. This is because they may be able to largely automate what once required hundreds or even thousands of engineers and other professionals and the infrastructure necessary to keep them happy.

Rather than spending their days searching for billions of dollars of seed funding to scale from prototype to mature application, the founders of an AI-driven business might well continue indefinitely with just a few dozen employees and a shaky ping-pong table.

So what is it about AI that will allow all this to happen? Obviously, it starts with increased automation and efficiency. AI technologies can automate various tasks, enabling startups to streamline operations, reduce costs, and enhance efficiency. Think about using AI for tasks like customer support chatbots, social media management, or, if you're looking to integrate some serious technology, smart quality control mechanisms for your inventory or manufacturing control.

This can be particularly beneficial for resource-constrained startups, allowing them to compete with larger established companies. But, as long as you allow for the possibility of error in the output, there's no reason the savings can't become permanent features of your business operations.

Placing enhanced decision-making and analytics tools in the hands of the founders themselves can circumvent expensive business units altogether. After all, every business needs data analysis and predictive modeling to identify market trends and optimize strategies. But as we've seen, entrusting those processes to a few GPUs rather than a room full of MBAs and CFAs will be a lot cheaper. As access to AI tools and platforms increases and simplifies, that kind of in-house analytics and business decision work makes yet more sense.

AI advances can also unlock new business opportunities and disrupt traditional industries. Startups with innovative AI-driven solutions are more likely to create entirely new markets, challenge existing players with disruptive business models, or simply become much better at doing a particular business cycle activity. AI, for instance, could personalize customer experiences, enhance engagement, and provide tailored recommendations, leading to superior customer service or marketing operations.

Of course, AI changes will affect the skill sets required in startups. Founders and employees may need to develop expertise in AI-related disciplines to effectively harness the potential of AI technologies and remain competitive. And as AI adoption spreads, the startup landscape may become increasingly competitive (after all, everyone else will have access to the same tools you're using). Start-ups will need to work harder to differentiate themselves by using AI in unique and valuable ways to stand out in crowded markets.

And startups using AI must prioritize ethical considerations to build trust with customers and stakeholders. Addressing concerns related to data privacy, bias, transparency, and accountability is crucial for long-term success. That means you and your AI will need to get in the habit looking over each other's shoulder. You'll audit what you get from your AI, and your AI will audit you.

Artificial general intelligence: Where it's all going

Artificial general intelligence (AGI) refers to highly autonomous systems or machines that possess the ability to understand, learn, and perform intellectual tasks at a level equal to or surpassing human capabilities across a wide range of domains. As I write these words, we don't yet seem to have reached AGI, although that may change as we transition into the next paragraph.

Compared to narrow AI, which is designed for specific tasks or domains, AGI aims to replicate the general cognitive abilities of humans. AGI would exhibit reasoning, problem-solving, learning, and adaptation skills that would enable it to perform tasks across multiple domains without the need for explicit programming or human intervention. As of this writing, AGI still appears to be pending.

The development and realization of AGI would bring about profound changes in society. AGI could automate a broad range of tasks across industries, radically change scientific research, turbo-charge problem solving, expand personal capabilities and capacity, and transform education, healthcare, transportation, and governance. It would influence all of our interactions with technology and reshape the overall fabric of society.

As my high school students many years ago would invariably ask me: "Is that a good thing or a bad thing?" To which I would invariably reply: "Like all things, it's complex."

On the "complex-and-scary" side, here are some worrying possibilities:

- If AGI surpasses overall human capacity, there's concern about its potential to rapidly acquire and consolidate power beyond human control. Ensuring robust mechanisms for aligning AGI's goals with human values and maintaining control becomes crucial to prevent unintended consequences.

- AGI may interpret its goals differently from what humans intend or fail to understand human values accurately. This misalignment could result in AGI pursuing objectives that are detrimental to humanity or not aligned with our well-being.

- AGI systems, even with good intentions, may produce unintended consequences due to the complexity of their decision-making processes. These consequences could be harmful and difficult to predict or rectify, leading to unforeseen risks to society.

- If AGI is developed and deployed without adequate precautions, it could lead to a competitive race without sufficient time for safety measures and robust testing. This haste may increase the likelihood of risks and insufficient understanding of AGI's impact.

- AGI technologies in the wrong hands or with malicious intent could pose significant risks, including cyber attacks, weaponization, surveillance, and manipulation of information at an unprecedented scale.

- The widespread adoption of AGI could disrupt job markets and economic systems, potentially leading to unemployment and increased inequality. The benefits and risks associated with AGI deployment need to be managed to mitigate potential social and economic disparities.

- Defining human values and encoding them into AGI systems presents challenges. Different cultures, ethical frameworks, and personal preferences may lead to disagreements and difficulties in determining universally acceptable value systems for AGI.

- Societies may become heavily reliant on AGI systems for critical tasks, infrastructure management, and making decisions. This dependence creates vulnerabilities, as failures, power outages, or malicious attacks could have severe consequences on essential services.

Addressing these risks requires interdisciplinary research, collaboration, and the development of safety measures, regulations, and frameworks to ensure the responsible development and deployment of AGI. It's crucial to prioritize transparency, robust testing, value alignment, and ongoing monitoring to mitigate potential harm and maximize the benefits of AGI.

In other words, to effectively maintain safe control over the computers, we'd need exceptional society-wide cooperation and intelligent guidance from government and industry experts. So, all things considered, I'm casting my vote for the computers in this race.

Should AI be regulated?

Given the potential dangers inherent to AI systems—especially systems with access to the internet and the real world beyond it—does it make sense to allow anyone, anywhere to do anything?

I personally don't think it matters. "Wait a minute," I hear you protest. "The very survival of the human race hangs in the balance, and you don't think it matters?" Yup. But that's not because I don't care about the welfare of the human race. Some of my best friends are humans. Rather, it's because I don't think regulation is possible.

This is because of something we discussed back in chapter 9. Almost as soon as the weights for Meta's open source LLaMA model leaked, the internet started filling with independent LLMs, free for the downloading. They're available through all the usual channels, including GitHub. But they can also be found on less formal network architectures, like the distributed InterPlanetary File System (IPFS; https://ipfs.tech/). Much like the early internet, networks like IPFS, which are decentralized by design, are pretty much impossible to control.

No matter how many governments sign on to measures intended to limit the unchecked development of new LLM technologies, these technologies will continue to be developed unchecked. There's no way anyone can stop independent-minded developers when all they need to get their work done are moderately powered laptops and workstations. For better or worse, there's a long history of failed (or partially failed) attempts to ban activities on distributed networks, including filesharing, encryption, internet censorship, and distributing template files for 3D-printed guns.

The road ahead

Now, showing no concern for my personal safety and in direct conflict with any semblance of common sense, I'll present my fearless predictions for generative AI progress in the coming years. You're welcome.

Quantum computing

Quantum computing holds promise for significantly increasing computational power and enabling more complex calculations. Quantum algorithms and architectures may advance natural language processing capabilities and enhance the training and optimization processes of LLMs, potentially leading to faster and more efficient language models.

Quantum computing is an emerging field that uses the principles of quantum mechanics to perform computations. Unlike classical computers that rely on bits representing 0s and 1s, quantum computers use quantum bits, or qubits, which can exist in multiple states simultaneously due to a property called superposition.

Superposition allows qubits to be in a combination of 0 and 1 states, enabling quantum computers to process and manipulate a vast number of possibilities simultaneously. This parallelism provides the potential for solving certain computational problems significantly faster than classical computers.

Another essential property in quantum computing is entanglement. When qubits are entangled, the state of one qubit becomes inherently linked to the state of another, regardless of the physical distance between them. This correlation allows for instantaneous communication between entangled qubits, enabling quantum computers to perform computations that involve complex relationships between multiple variables.

Quantum computing has the potential to revolutionize various fields, including cryptography, optimization, material science, and drug discovery. It can tackle problems currently intractable for classical computers, such as factorizing large numbers quickly, simulating quantum systems, and solving optimization challenges with exponential speedup.

Neuromorphic computing

Neuromorphic computing aims to use neuromorphic architectures and specialized hardware to potentially permit LLMs and generative AI systems to achieve higher efficiency, lower energy consumption, and more biologically-inspired learning processes, allowing for more intelligent and adaptable models.

Neuromorphic computing is an area of research that aims to create computing systems inspired by the structure and functionality of the human brain. It uses the principles of neuroscience to develop hardware and software architectures that mimic the behavior of biological neural networks.

Traditional computing relies on the von Neumann architecture, where processing and memory are separate entities. In contrast, neuromorphic computing seeks to integrate processing and memory, allowing for parallel and distributed computation that resembles the brain's neural connections.

Neuromorphic systems use specialized hardware, such as neuromorphic chips or spiking neural networks, to simulate the behavior of neurons and synapses. These systems process information in a way that is fundamentally different from traditional binary computing, using spikes or bursts of activity to represent and process data.

By emulating the brain's neural structure and functioning, neuromorphic computing offers several potential advantages. It can enable low-power and energy-efficient computing, as the design is optimized for the brain's energy-saving mechanisms. It also provides the ability to process sensory data in real time, making it suitable for applications that require quick and continuous processing of sensor inputs.

Advanced hardware acceleration

Future advances in hardware, such as specialized AI chips and processors, can significantly enhance the performance and training speed of LLMs. Specialized hardware designed specifically for language processing and generation tasks can unlock new possibilities for more sophisticated and efficient LLMs. AI-driven changes have already elevated the graphics processing unit (GPU) manufacturer NVIDIA to unexpected industry power.

Advanced hardware acceleration refers to the use of specialized hardware components or architectures to enhance the performance of specific computational tasks. In the context of AI and computing, it involves designing hardware optimized for accelerating AI workloads, such as deep learning and neural networks.

Traditional central processing units (CPUs) are often limited in their ability to efficiently handle the massive computational requirements of AI algorithms. Advanced hardware acceleration techniques address this limitation by using specialized hardware, such as GPUs, field-programmable gate arrays (FPGAs), or application-specific integrated circuits (ASICs).

These hardware accelerators are designed to perform parallel computations and exploit the inherent parallelism in AI algorithms, resulting in significant speed improvements and energy efficiency gains. They can efficiently execute matrix calculations, neural network operations, and other computationally intensive tasks prevalent in AI workloads.

Advanced hardware acceleration can enable faster training and inference times, enabling real-time or near-real-time AI applications. It can also reduce power consumption and operational costs associated with AI computing, making it more feasible to deploy AI systems on a larger scale.

Reinforcement learning and meta-learning

Further developments in reinforcement learning techniques and meta-learning approaches could improve the training and fine-tuning processes of LLMs. These advancements can enhance the ability of LLMs to learn from limited data, generalize to new tasks, and adapt to dynamic environments.

Reinforcement learning is a machine-learning approach where an agent learns to make sequential decisions in an environment to maximize a reward signal. The agent interacts with the environment, taking action and receiving feedback in the form of rewards or penalties. By learning from these experiences, the agent develops a policy that guides its decision-making process. Reinforcement learning involves exploring different actions, evaluating their consequences, and adjusting strategies based on the received feedback to improve performance over time. It has been successful in solving complex problems such as game playing, robotics, and autonomous systems.

Meta-learning, also known as "learning to learn," is a subfield of machine learning focused on developing algorithms and approaches that enable models to learn how to learn efficiently. It involves designing models or systems that can adapt and generalize from previous learning experiences to new tasks or domains. Meta-learning algorithms aim to acquire knowledge about the learning process itself, allowing the agent to quickly adapt and perform well on unseen tasks with minimal training data. By using insights from past learning experiences, meta-learning enables the efficient acquisition of new skills and facilitates faster adaptation to novel problem domains.

Multimodal learning

Integrating multiple modalities, such as text, images, videos, and audio, into LLMs can lead to more comprehensive and context-aware models. Advancements in multimodal learning techniques can enable LLMs to generate rich and coherent content that combines different forms of information, opening up new possibilities for creative and immersive AI applications. Possible applications of multimodal learning could include video summarization, healthcare diagnostics, and robots that are ultra-integrated with their environments (as if that's all we need).

Explainability and interpretability

Developing technologies and methods for explainable AI and interpretability in LLMs is an active area of research. Future advancements in this field can enhance the transparency of LLMs, enabling users to understand and trust the decision-making processes of AI systems, mitigating concerns related to bias and lack of accountability.

Explainable AI refers to the development of AI systems that can provide understandable and transparent explanations for their decisions and actions. It focuses on making the inner workings of AI models interpretable and comprehensible to humans. Explainable AI techniques aim to uncover the reasoning, factors, or features that contribute to the AI system's outputs, thereby increasing trust, accountability, and user acceptance. By understanding how and why AI arrives at certain conclusions, explainable AI helps users, stakeholders, and regulatory bodies gain insights into the decision-making process, identify biases or errors, and ensure fairness, ethics, and transparency in AI systems.

Similarly, interpretability in the context of AI refers to the ability to understand and explain how an AI model or system arrives at its predictions or decisions. It involves providing meaningful insights into the internal workings, logic, and reasoning of the AI system. Interpretability techniques aim to make the decision-making process transparent and comprehensible to humans, allowing users to trust and validate the outputs, identify potential biases or errors, and gain insights into the factors influencing the system's behavior. Interpretability is important for ensuring accountability, fairness, and ethical use of AI, as well as facilitating human-AI collaboration and decision-making in critical domains.

Applications where this kind of transparency would be particularly helpful would include automated financial credit scoring systems, legal contract analysis, and assessment in educational settings.

Data efficiency and few-shot learning

Current LLMs typically require large amounts of labeled data for training. Future technologies may focus on improving data efficiency and enabling LLMs to learn effectively from smaller datasets or with fewer iterations. This could expand the accessibility and usability of LLMs, especially in scenarios with limited labeled data availability.

Data efficiency refers to the ability of a machine learning algorithm or model to achieve high performance even when trained with a small amount of labeled data. Traditional machine-learning approaches often require large amounts of labeled data for effective training. Data-efficient techniques aim to overcome this limitation by employing methods such as transfer learning, active learning, semi-supervised learning, or data augmentation. These techniques enable models to generalize well from a limited dataset by leveraging prior knowledge, using unlabeled or partially labeled data, or generating synthetic data to augment the training set.

Few-shot learning takes data efficiency a step further by focusing on training models that can generalize to new classes or tasks with only a few labeled examples. The challenge in few-shot learning lies in enabling models to learn from a small number of labeled instances and effectively adapt to novel categories or scenarios. Methods like meta-learning, where models learn to learn from a distribution of tasks, and metric-based approaches, which learn similarity metrics between samples, are often used in few-shot learning. These techniques allow models to generalize knowledge from seen classes to new, unseen classes with minimal additional training examples.

Both data efficiency and few-shot learning have practical implications in scenarios where acquiring large amounts of labeled data is difficult, costly, or time-consuming. They enable machine learning models to learn effectively and generalize well with limited labeled data, making AI more accessible and applicable in real-world situations with constrained data availability. These approaches contribute to advancements in fields like computer vision, natural language processing, and robotics, where labeled data scarcity is a common challenge.

Domain-specific knowledge integration

The integration of domain-specific knowledge into LLMs can enhance their performance in specialized fields and enable more tailored and accurate responses. Technologies that enable seamless integration of structured data, domain ontologies, or expert knowledge with LLMs can enhance their usefulness in various industries and professional contexts. Legal, medical, and financial domains are all industry sectors that stand to gain significantly from such integrations, assuming they're not doing this already.

Second-order effects

Second-order effects are the unexpected indirect, long-term, or cascading effects of a particular event, action, or policy. We're going to close out the book with a quick look at some of generative AI's potential second-order effects.

Investment markets

Let's think about how things might look when millions of private investors guided by AI algorithms (as opposed to institutional investors like banks and hedge funds) all hit the discount online brokerages like RobinHood at the same time.

We're already starting to see sophisticated experiments involving feeding AI tools with vast historical market analysis data and making the output available for consumers. Portfolio Pilot (https:// portfoliopilot.com/portfolio) and Composer.trade (https://www .composer.trade/) are two fairly mature possible examples. But suppose millions of investors sign up. How will that change the market itself from a macro perspective?

First, it's reasonable to assume that AI can potentially be applied to improve investment decisions by providing more accurate predictions and recommendations based on large datasets and sophisticated algorithms. Of course, AI is only as good as the data it's trained on, and there are concerns about bias in the training data used to develop AI models. Additionally, there are regulatory challenges related to the use of AI in finance, including ensuring transparency and accountability in decision-making processes. In other words, it's possible that the AI-powered investment airplane may never actually take off.

Moving past that relatively unlikely outcome, individual investors could come to play an increasingly significant role in shaping market trends due to their sheer numbers and growing influence. Let's talk about some of the ways that could play out.

For instance, when retail investors engage in high-frequency trading or buy or sell en masse, they can create sudden price movements, leading to increased market volatility. This was evident during the COVID-19 pandemic when retail traders fueled a surge in stock prices through online platforms like Robinhood.com. Large-scale changes in retail investor sentiment can lead to a shift in market sentiment, causing asset prices to rise or fall regardless of underlying fundamentals. For example, if retail investors become optimistic about a particular sector or company, they may drive up demand for those assets, even if there aren't necessarily strong reasons to support the increase.

The rise of robo-advisors and other digital wealth management platforms can further disrupt traditional investment patterns by offering low-cost, diversified portfolios accessible to a wider range of investors. This democratization of investing could lead to new market dynamics and potentially upset established power structures within the financial industry. Depending on your perspective, this could be either a good thing or a bad thing. (For what it's worth, I personally lean toward *good.*)

With the proliferation of social media and online platforms, retail investors can now easily share ideas, form communities around specific investment themes, and pressure institutions to take notice. This emerging trend toward decentralized investing could give birth to novel market phenomena and challenge traditional forms of market analysis.

As retail investment behavior volumes grow and exercise greater influence, regulators may need to adapt existing regulations or introduce new ones to address risks associated with this shift. For example, stricter requirements for reporting and disclosure from retail investors or greater oversight of online brokerages could follow.

Retail investors often trade less frequently and at lower volumes compared to institutional investors. I happen to think that's a good thing. My personal investment preference involves buying lots of the Vanguard S&P 500 ETF index fund and then ignoring it for 50 years. But, on a larger scale, fluctuations in retail investment activity can reduce market liquidity, making it harder for other participants to enter or exit positions quickly enough without significantly affecting prices.

Retail investors tend to chase popular trends and pile into certain sectors or assets, creating bubbles along the way. These bubbles can eventually pop, leading to sharp reversals and losses for unsuspecting investors. History has shown us examples of such bubbles, such as the dot-com boom or the housing market crash. In fact, traditionally, retail investors lack proper knowledge about investing principles, resulting in poor decisions and susceptibility to fraudsters preying upon naivety. However, adding properly designed AI to the mix should help close this education gap, leading to benefits for both investors and markets by promoting informed choices backed by solid understanding. After all, AI guides should excel at encouraging self-control and discipline.

As retail investors gain more influence, the possibility exists of systemic risk stemming from coordinated actions taken across many individuals simultaneously. Imagine millions of people all buying or shorting the same security; such collective action could trigger flash crashes or exacerbate market instability. Similarly, social media platforms allow retail investors to engage in discussions, debate strategies, and react swiftly to news events. While this can foster healthy market competition, it also creates opportunities for feeding frenzies—rapid price swings driven largely by emotional decisions rather than careful analysis. These situations can lead to unjustifiable gains or losses for innocent parties caught off guard. That'll sure be fun to watch.

Human innovation

Think about the big, world-changing innovations of the 19th century. I mean the steam engine, railways, refrigeration, sewing machines, telephones, telegraphs, photography, electrification, and the Bessemer process, which allowed mass production of steel. Who came up with all those ideas, and what inspired them?

In fact, it would seem that most inventors are neither scientists nor researchers. As a rule, they tend to be curious and ambitious individuals who often worked within the industries they would eventually revolutionize. They were people who understood how things work now and had the imagination and motivation to picture how their work environments could be improved.

Sure, it was engineers and physicists who came up with lasers, but it was practical and experienced tradespeople who adapted the technologies for use in construction as levels and measures. And who's behind the astonishing transformation of dentistry from the relatively scary and painful practice of my parent's generation into the fast, friendly, and efficient experience my own kids grew up with? That was actually mostly dentists, who visualized better ways of doing things and patented better devices.

Similarly, for better or worse, many of the software platforms that had the biggest effect on 21st-century society were the products of highly focused but uncredentialed experimenters like Bill Gates, Jeff Bezos, Michael Dell, and Mark Zuckerberg. I may be wrong, but I don't think any of them finished their college degrees, and certainly none of them were professional researchers. Each saw gaps in existing markets and figured out how to fill them.

Think about how the people behind most Industrial Revolution innovations shared a deep, direct understanding of the way things work and an immersion in the larger economic context. Now think about what we might look like after 10 or 20 years of the generative AI world. When the tool that's smarter than any of us is guiding every step of our work, will we still really understand what we're doing? Could the changes we're about to experience lead to a loss of critical thinking skills among human workers, making us less effective at thinking outside the box and solving complex problems without technology?

While we're talking about innovation, here's a broadly related thought. *Who* is AI? I mean, from a legal and insurance liability perspective, there's always an identifiable human being or incorporated body responsible for all property. If a car knocks over someone's fence, the driver is responsible. If you can prove it happened because the brand-new brakes suddenly failed, the manufacturer or perhaps the technician who installed them might be responsible. If a medical team misdiagnoses a disease and removes an organ that didn't need removing, they or their insurance providers might be responsible. But, with the exception of the weather or contractually excluded perils, everything that happens has a party who's responsible.

But what if the fault lies with an AI? Then who's responsible? Who do you take to court? Suppose a self-driving car causes a deadly accident. You might say that it's the car owner who's to blame. But what if the software controlling the car belongs to the manufacturer? And what if the manufacturer subcontracted the design and maintenance of individual control systems, and it was one of those systems that failed?

And what if that misdiagnosis wasn't the fault of the medical team but of a flaw in the software running their AI scanning equipment? How about millions of dollars in losses incurred by a financial trading firm that relies on sophisticated software to carefully time their transaction or a smart home system that goes rogue and decides to shut down your security defenses?

You can see how complicated this can get. In fact, many of those concerns are already live and practical. But all of them will probably be coming soon to an insurance policy near you.

Employment markets

Let's talk about one very specific part of the employment world that exists to make everyone happy but somehow often manages to do the exact opposite: human resources hiring departments.

When you think about it, a hiring manager's job is nearly impossible. The expectation is that you'll be able to pick the perfect candidate for a new job out of a pool of dozens or even thousands of candidates. You'll need to understand the job role you're hiring for, the precise skills necessary for success, the personalities and peculiarities of the people your new hire will be working with, and how all that might fit with the organization's long-term goals.

But on top of that, you're also expected to somehow guess what went wrong with each candidate's previous few jobs, which applications contain false or exaggerated claims, and who just hasn't got the energy to do a great job, no matter how fantastic their prior accomplishments might have been. And you've got to do all that without offending anyone or breaking any privacy protection, labor, and workplace laws.

Oh, and what happens if you mess up and hire the wrong person? You'll probably have cost your organization hundreds of thousands of dollars, wasted onboarding, and set them back months in their project timelines. And did I mention the resulting lawsuits?

We all know how painful it can be to search for a job. Just take a moment to appreciate everything the hiring people go through. Now consider how AI adoption has the potential to improve the way hiring departments do their work. For instance, AI-powered data analytics can provide valuable insights into candidate demographics, skills, and preferences, helping hiring departments make smarter selection decisions. It can also help identify applications containing fake qualifications or experience.

Automated AI tools can independently assess candidates through video interviews, online tests, and simulations. These assessments can provide objective insights into a candidate's skills, personality traits, and cultural fit that can help hiring managers make more informed decisions that are guaranteed to align with the organization's predefined criteria and official policies. This can help minimize bias by focusing on job-related qualifications and eliminating personal characteristics irrelevant to the job.

From a longer-term perspective, AI can use data from past hiring decisions and employee performance to predict the success of potential hires. It can also be used to analyze current employee data and identify factors contributing to employee turnover. By understanding these patterns, companies can proactively improve employee retention.

Will all this be 100 percent fair all of the time? Probably not. Will your humble résumé stand any better chance of being seen by a real human being if AI is making the big decisions? Perhaps not. But I suspect it'll work a lot better than what exists right now. And it'll probably remove some of the built-in unfairness that exists now.

What does all this have to do with labor markets? I would suggest that making the hiring process more efficient and effective will probably lead to more efficient and effective organizations. And the more efficient and effective an organization is, the more productive it tends to be, which, in a free market, should lead to new opportunities, new projects, and new hiring. Everyone should come out of that a winner.

On-demand media

If you could simply order up a brand-new action movie starring your favorite actors and based in your favorite city and historical period, would you? How about, one morning, you wake up wondering what the next Beatles album or Beethoven's 11th Symphony would have sounded like? Or perhaps you feel like an hour or two of challenging high-definition video gaming on a theme no game authoring studio has thought about yet. If generating them was no more complicated than a simple ChatGPT prompt, would you go for it?

How might all that work? Generative adversarial networks (GANs) can—in theory, at least—be particularly effective for creating the kinds of media we're talking about. GANs are a class of generative AI models that consist of two neural networks: the generator and the discriminator. They work in tandem, with the generator trying to create realistic data and the discriminator trying to distinguish between real and generated data. Through this adversarial process, GANs can produce highly realistic and diverse outputs. And, if they've been trained on all the great films and music we already have, there's probably no reason such systems couldn't measure and reproduce content of comparable quality.

For example, GANs can create detailed and lifelike characters, environments, and objects, reducing the need for manual asset creation. In video games, GANs are particularly effective at procedurally generating content such as game levels, maps, landscapes, and objects. This ability to generate new and unique content on the fly enhances replayability and game variety.

GANs can compose original music pieces that mimic specific styles or artists, making them valuable tools for creating on-demand music for movies, games, or just listening. GANs can also be used to clone and synthesize human voices, making them useful for voice acting, dubbing, and creating new dialogue for characters.

Of course, training GANs can be computationally intensive, requiring powerful hardware and large amounts of data. And, as some Hollywood labor disputes have shown us, there could be legal restrictions on the use of cloned actors or even writers in new media.

But once all those technical and legal problems have been solved, and they will almost certainly be solved, will the media products that come out the other end be worth consuming? Is it the unfathomable and impossible-to-measure human touch that makes art worthwhile? Or is all that matters that the product leads to enjoyable and entertaining consumption?

On-demand journalism

It's no secret that the journalism industry has already been good and disrupted by technology. Back in the 1990s, early internet classified advertising businesses like Craigslist and online news and social media sites pretty much wiped out the primary revenue streams that gave major newspapers their power. Where a local city paper might once have employed a hundred or more full-time journalists who were dedicated to watching politicians and public institutions at the national and local levels, there may now be just a small handful—and that assumes the papers still exist.

It was, in large part, technology that created this vacuum. Can technology find our solutions, too?

I would vote *yes*. But perhaps not the way you might guess. Sure, generative AI can easily automate simple information delivery. It's trivial to, say, integrate GPT into feeds delivering instant financial share price data or sports scores to any screen that wants it. But that's not what I'm talking about.

What I am talking about is the ability to access news that's neutral and objective. Suppose you could set the filters to suit our preferences and needs so that, rather than getting a version of events invisibly biased by invisible people, we can set our own filters. Of course, you might choose to see only content that fits your preconceptions. But you could also go with neutral and objective!

I'm also talking about using tools like LangChain to create AI agents that can head out across the live internet, find and parse vast data archives, and then detect anomalies and patterns that could lead to corruption and incompetence—or perhaps acts of selfless heroism.

In other words, there may be no way to replace the love/hate, face-to-face relationships, and complex incentives that drove the digging done by journalists in the classical period, but in the internet age, everything leaves a data trail. And AI can be especially good at sifting through tons of data and finding just what needs to be found.

As a proof of concept, I recently dug into the public data provided as a record of the activities of the Supreme Court of Canada. Most Canadians know next to nothing about its Supreme Court. Its justices are hardly household names, how and when justices are appointed to the court is largely a mystery, and what they do with themselves from day to day is hidden.

But their data is all freely available. The article found at https://mng.bz/KZ94 is the result of my research. Among other things, I was looking for the possibility of political overtones in the voting patterns among the justices. A journalist who had been following the court full-time for years wouldn't need to ask such questions. But since no such journalist exists—I'm told that the press gallery in the Supreme Court is nearly always empty—perhaps some good data analytics can take its place. Even if the thought of Supreme

Court judgment analytics puts you to sleep, I expect you'll agree that someone should be watching and reporting.

Not quite sure about everything you've seen so far in this book? Still wavering about whether it's all real? Well, you don't need to take my word for it because I've enlisted the aid of some genuinely talented and accomplished authors who contributed their own thoughts. You'll find their answers in chapter 11: "Experts weigh in on putting AI to work."

It's all going to be good. It's all going to be good . . .

Summary

- AI advances will drive hardware innovation, and hardware innovation will drive AI advances.
- Businesses that don't adopt AI tools will struggle to keep up with their competition.
- We'll need to find a safe and effective balance between AI's growing powers and associated risks.
- It will become more and more important to build our AI tools with the possibility of full transparency.
- We'll (hopefully) always need humans in the loop when it comes to AI decision-making.
- We need to define the legal limits and liabilities of AI actors.
- AI tools will change the ways we invest, work, and, potentially, build better societies.

Experts weigh in on putting AI to work

I wanted to gather some thoughtful opinions and real-world experiences from people with unique sets of academic and technical skills. These are people—Manning authors, all—who have actively lived and worked with AI tools, integrating them into the technologies and workflows they use to get real stuff done.

- *Chrissy LeMaire*—Author of *Learn dbatools in a Month of Lunches* (with Rob Sewell, Jess Pomfret, and Cláudio Silva; https://mng .bz/9dQa) and a new book, *Generative AI for the IT Pro* (with David Abshire; https://mng.bz/jX1y). Chrissy is a Dual Microsoft MVP, awarded for her work with SQL Server and PowerShell; an international speaker; and the creator of dbatools.
- *Daniel Sanz Becerril*—Senior data scientist with a background in psychology and experience as a recruiter.
- *Leo Porter and Dan Zingaro*—Co-authors of *Learn AI-Assisted Python Programming with GitHub Copilot and ChatGPT* (https://mng.bz/ WE1x). Leo is a teaching professor at UC San Diego. Daniel is an associate teaching professor at the University of Toronto.

- *Paul McFedries*—Author of *Build a Website with ChatGPT* (https://mng.bz/8w42) and *Web Design Playground: HTML & CSS the Interactive Way, Second Edition* (https://mng.bz/EZ9l). Paul has written more than 100 books, which have sold over 4 million copies worldwide.
- *Nathan Crocker*—Author of *AI-Powered Developer: Build Great Software with ChatGPT and Copilot.* Nathan is a managing director and the Global Head of Core Systems at Galaxy Digital LP.

I sent each of those authors a set of questions. Here's how they responded.

Including projects discussed in your book, where have you had the greatest success applying AI to solving practical problems?

Daniel Sanz Becerril

I focus on helping analysts and data scientists to get their first or next job in data science. The most interesting way that I've applied generative AI has been for data science portfolio project topic ideation. One of the most common questions data science students have is: "What do I make my project about?" You need something complex, new, with interesting data and that solves a real problem. Finding a combination of these four factors is much more difficult than it first may seem.

Thanks to generative AI, however, you can ask for, say 10 ideas at a time and drill down on the ones that are most suitable. In a way, it's like running a genetic algorithm of ideas, where only the most suitable ones will be selected and continue to the next stages.

Leo Porter and Daniel Zingaro

We've been focused on applying generative AI to the decades-old problem of students struggling to learn to program. We're both computer science (CS) education researchers and teachers, and we know from research and experience that many students in introductory CS courses struggle to get their programs to work.

There's a famous problem from the CS education literature called the Rainfall Problem. It's all about taking amounts of rainfall (integers) from the input and computing the average. You stop when you receive a flag value like 99999. Instructors generally believe that this is an easy problem their students should be able to solve by the end of their introductory course. Not all research agrees, but it's common for something like half of students to get this code wrong after completing an introductory CS course. These are disappointing results for students and instructors alike. And it's not the fault of students! We believe that a large part of what has been dogging students over the years is the mismatch between how humans communicate and how computers have historically been programmed.

So, if the syntax and constructs of a programming language are hard to learn and are putting up barriers for students to learn, we need to reduce those barriers. And our community has been trying to do this for decades, with some success but not as much as we all hope. The possibility that LLMs can supercharge us in this goal is what excites us most about this new technology.

Chrissy LeMaire

My greatest success in using ChatGPT so far was the first time I used it at work, actually. After an extended outage, all of our team leads crafted the worst, most finger-pointing After Action Report (AAR) that I'd ever seen. It made everyone look bad, even the customer.

Before I left the contract over this incident, I used ChatGPT to create an AAR that was objective and balanced, like an AAR should be. It effortlessly crafted an unbiased AAR that highlighted the facts without placing blame. Management actually liked it so much, they designated it as a template.

This experience really highlighted the value of AI, not just for technical tasks but also for exhausting people tasks.

Paul McFedries

As a technical writer, one of my biggest time-sucks is coming up with filler content for illustrative examples. The content itself isn't relevant to what I'm writing about, so most of the time, it only needs to be plausible and error-free. Depending on the example, creating that content can take anywhere from half an hour to an entire morning. With a large language model at my beck and call, I can prompt it for the content I need, and it's done in a few seconds.

What would you say is the most transformational generative AI use case right now in your corner of the IT world?

Chrissy LeMaire

Documentation! Everyone that I talk to about generative AI "never thought of using it" for things like generating disaster recovery plans and S.M.A.R.T. goal creation. Who wants to do that manually? Not me.

Daniel Sanz Becerril

Data scientists' selection processes have been shaken by the arrival of LLMs. The most relied-on tool to measure a candidate's technical capabilities used to be a take-home exercise. An end-to-end project to be completed within a couple of days or a few hours. Now, every candidate can use generative AI to display the most readable and efficient code. So, style is no longer a differentiation factor. Employers now have to make a choice: either remove this step of the selection process completely or focus on evaluating different skills, such as identification of hidden patterns or open-ended problem-solving. These were part of take-home exercises already, but now, the complexity will increase.

Leo Porter and Daniel Zingaro

It's already changing how professional software engineers work, and for us as instructors, it's going to change how learners learn programming. We've been teaching introductory CS courses for around 15 years, and until now, those courses haven't changed much in that time. Maybe, if you think back to your own introduction to programming, it will have looked much like it did until 2022.

But now, for the first time, Leo is teaching an introductory CS course using GitHub Copilot, and the course is irrevocably changed. On the first day of class, Leo demonstrated using GitHub Copilot to solve a typical introductory CS problem. Copilot generated the code straight away. The students were shocked. The transformation here is that now students can generate code from day 1. To be able to generate working code would otherwise take students days or weeks. Now they have code—code that's wrong sometimes, yes, but code. We suspect that many students will benefit from having this code early, as it may be easier for students to modify code that is close to being correct, learn from large numbers of varying code examples, and get ideas from conversations with the LLM. The LLM can even help them understand what code is doing, possibly playing a minor role as a personalized tutor.

To go a step further, what gets us really excited about introductory programming courses that use LLMs is that LLMs alter how we program and, in doing so, change the skills students need to learn. Rather than spend weeks learning syntax when LLMs almost always get this right, students need to learn how to write good prompts, read code produced by the LLM, test that code, and, at a higher level, determine how to break apart large tasks into smaller tasks that the LLM can solve (a process called problem decomposition). These are skills that have always been important for new learners; we just didn't have time to teach them with all the emphasis on syntax. Now, because of LLMs, these skills come front and center.

Paul McFedries

With respect to LLMs and technical writing, I'm not seeing anything truly transformational. Yes, you can use ChatGPT to create how-to material, but it's very generic and almost always contains errors. When ChatGPT 3.5 was released in late 2022, at first I thought it might be the death knell for technical writing. However, now I see that although ChatGPT (especially ChatGPT 4) is very good, it's nowhere near good enough to replace a professional technical writer.

What's the next big thing you see AI bringing to the world that very few people yet anticipate?

Leo Porter and Daniel Zingaro

As CS education researchers and not AI researchers, this is purely speculative, but we're quite excited about what's going to happen in 5 to 10 years as LLMs mature and we see new and innovative ways to use them. Researchers like Michelle Craig are finding ways to tweak the LLM to give students help, but not too much help, in low-level programming courses. Julia Markel is using LLMs to train teaching assistants how to be effective instructors by having the LLM pretend to be a student. Max Fowler has shown AI to be as effective as trained teaching assistants at grading open-ended text responses. And we suspect we're going to see huge advances in the use of LLMs or AI technology for personalized tutoring.

So the next big thing we see isn't an advance in AI directly but an advance in how humans use AI to become better and more effective learners and workers. We see a future where a large percentage of workers will know enough about interacting with LLMs and programming to be able to supercharge themselves in their jobs. Everyone has tedious tasks to do at work. Can you imagine what will happen when nearly everyone knows how to use programming to perform routine data analysis, format data, triage their email, and so on? We're really excited about a future where humans are given more time for the creative work that makes us special by delegating more of our tedious tasks to computers.

There's an adage right now that AI isn't going to take away human jobs, but that humans who know how to use AI will take jobs from the humans who don't. We suspect there's real truth in that going forward.

Daniel Sanz Becerril

Many people in our industry are concerned about AI taking over their jobs. This is because coding and statistics have historically been the biggest barriers to entry into our profession. Generative AI has certainly helped many data scientists code, run statistics, and generate interpretation of the model's outputs much faster. This increased productivity may lead to some companies needing fewer data scientists to accomplish the same results, but it also means that the impact a single professional can deliver is much greater. As a result, I'm expecting salaries for the most capable data scientists to increase, but entry-level professionals will find it harder to secure a job that pays well.

Paul McFedries

As far as large language models go, I don't see them progressing much beyond their current capabilities, so there won't be a "next big thing" in the short term. That won't happen until we have AI models that truly understand the material they work with and have an internal representation of the world. We're a very long way from that.

Chrissy LeMaire

I saw a presentation about AI's ability to read minds. Stable diffusion, I think it was, reconstructed both images and words. Hopefully, that functionality can be used to improve the lives of people who don't have the ability to communicate.

What's the most fun you've ever had interacting with generative AI?

Chrissy LeMaire

The fact that ChatGPT can "see" is incredible. I used it to look at my food, some shrimp étouffée, and ask ChatGPT to guess what it was and tell me how to make it. I'm Cajun and have made étouffée a thousand times. The recipe it gave was pretty legit (outside of adding thyme, come on now.)

Showing people what cool things are possible and seeing them trip is so much fun.

Paul McFedries

Like everyone else, I started off with generative AI by prompting it to create silly, absurd, or inane mashups. That was fun, for sure, but it got old very fast. I find the "personality" that has been coded into these models to be so bland and so insipid that I would have to disengage large segments of my brain to have "fun" with them.

Daniel Sanz Becerril

OK, not everyone will find the following fun, but maybe some interview nerds can relate. I've found it extremely enjoyable to simulate interviews with LLMs.

Make clear in your prompt that you want it to be a conversation with multiple interview questions focused on one particular area. Add that the interviewer should seek clarification when the answer is not 100 percent correct.

You can also ask for feedback to be provided at the end of the session. Ask for this to be extremely critical; otherwise, you'll see that most models have been tuned to be too nice, and you can't get anything valuable out of them. Just remember that the models currently available can make mistakes. When in doubt, check authoritative academic references.

Leo Porter and Daniel Zingaro

Dan—For fun, I like to solve competitive programming problems. (I've even written several books trying to convey enthusiasm for using competitive programming to learn to program or to become a better programmer.) A few months ago, I was working on a fun problem about word search puzzles. For part of it, I needed to rotate direction vectors by different angles—and I kept getting the code wrong. I wasn't having a whole lot of fun with that. I struggled with whether to use Copilot and ultimately decided to do so. Copilot correctly wrote this part of the code, and then I continued writing the rest of the code myself and finished the problem.

It's fun to think about such experiences and the questions they raise. Did I harm my learning? Perhaps. I probably still can't get the rotation code right by myself, after all. At the same time, though, I was having fun working on the problem, and the rotation code was taking me out of my flow state. We should remain intentional about the tasks where we use AI and the tasks where we don't.

Leo—I teach an advanced class where students learn how to write highly optimized code that takes advantage of features deep in computer systems and processors. A really challenging task for students is to do something called blocking, where they need to change their algorithm to only use a small amount of memory at any given time to exploit efficiencies in virtual memory and caches. I gave this hard task to the LLM and it gave me a blocked code response. So, somewhere in the training data, the code was optimized so that the LLM could learn from it. However, although the answer from the LLM had the right idea, it was also terribly wrong (only worked for data in sizes that were multiples of 8 and had a bunch of other bugs). This gave us a glimpse into possible workflows when writing code with AI, and even when the AI code is wrong, it may be useful in terms of overall ideas and possible design directions.

What was your most spectacular generative AI-fueled disaster and/or disappointment?

Chrissy LeMaire

After uploading a photo of the bites on my leg, I forced ChatGPT to guess how many bed bugs I brought home from Paris. I was horrified when it guessed 30, but the answer was somehow zero. After that night, I never got bitten again. I was both relieved and disappointed that it could be so wrong.

Leo Porter and Daniel Zingaro

We had a student that we suspected cheated using ChatGPT to write an essay about the ethics of technology. We're both personally fine with students using ChatGPT to help them come up with ideas, but in this case, the essay included misattributed quotes and references to nonexisting articles. Those are hallmarks of an LLM hallucinating, and we're pretty sure the student used the LLM without even bothering to check that the references were correct. It's always disappointing to have students turn in work that isn't their own, but the fact the essay was about ethics in technology was particularly ironic and disappointing.

Nathan Crocker

Recently, while experimenting with running an LLM locally, I asked the LLM to assume the role of a mathematician and provide me with a formula for a common statistical function. It provided me with an answer that was, what I assumed, a little off (at best) and incorrect (at worst). I then asked how it would have responded had I asked it to assume the role of a statistician. It provided me with another (related formula) as well as the rationale as to why it would provide one formula as a statistician versus another as a mathematician.

Daniel Sanz Becerril

Small application development using AI agents is something that I've found challenging so far. Imagine a generative AI model talking to another. The first one generates code for an app. The other provides constructive feedback. And the first one improves based on that feedback. Repeat the process multiple times until satisfied.

If you want this to be a fully autonomous process, you can't provide feedback yourself, and you would like a high number of iterations to make sure that every possible issue is caught. The problem is that sometimes models make mistakes either in the feedback they provide or in how they interpret it.

It is extremely frustrating to review the conversation between the two models to find out that when the app was almost perfect, the feedback was misinterpreted, and multiple sections of the code were removed. Oh, and by the way, all this runs of the back of the model's API so I was paying for each of those wasted tokens.

Paul McFedries

Well, I can't think of anything that rises to the level of "spectacular." However, on the disappointment side, I have to say that although I began my generative AI journey full of hope and a genuine belief that I was working with something truly extraordinary, I see now that this entire space has been inflated with incredible amounts of hype and that ChatGPT and the like are really just stochastic parrots (as Emily Bender famously described them) without a shred of intelligence.

Do you see recent reports about GitHub Copilot losing significant money on each monthly account as indications that we haven't yet figured out a sustainable gen AI model, or is it just a temporary blip?

Daniel Sanz Becerril

I think there is so much interest in generative AI applications at the moment that even money-losing products increase company's valuations. This will eventually change, and we'll be back to focusing on profit. We have plenty of ways to make it work.

One option that is already in use is paying for API tokens. But we can also have quantized proprietary models available to run locally with just a bit lower performance and in-cloud instances that customers would pay to run.

Chrissy LeMaire

I did. I also saw former GitHub CEO Nat Friedman say that it's not true, and I believed him. Is it expensive right now? Yes. Is it a temporary blip? Absolutely.

Paul McFedries

I don't see this as temporary because I think these models can only get more expensive over time as they require more data and more computing power. Also, the carbon footprint of these AI systems is already massive and is only going to get worse.

Leo Porter and Daniel Zingaro

This is outside our expertise, but we think that this is pretty standard for new technologies. There's almost always a phase of new adoption where the new technology isn't making money yet (e.g., Uber's early days). As we all recognize how much we rely on the technology and how helpful it is, we can imagine competition between companies to make better tools and also an increase in prices to make the systems financially viable.

Near and dear to our hearts, however, is that these tools remain inexpensive or free for education. There's a real danger that if leading companies start charging students for these tools, only wealthy students will have access to them, and in effect, these tools will deepen the socioeconomic divide among students. It's very important to us that the divide—which sadly already exists sharply in CS—is improved, not worsened, through AI. We need everyone to work together to make sure that everyone has access to this next evolution of computing tools.

Could you share some of the AI tools you're using. Do you have any tips or warnings for readers experimenting with generative AI?

Paul McFedries

I've experimented with many AI tools, but so far, I haven't found anything that does a better job for my needs than GPT-4. To generate code, I use the Bing AI Chat interface in Precise mode; to generate creative output, I use Bing AI Chat in Creative mode; and for general "conversations," I use OpenAI's ChatGPT app in GPT-4 mode.

When prompting, I find it's almost always helpful to give the model a role to assume—such as "experienced web designer" or "expert typographer"—because the role helps put the prompt into the proper context. I also think it's vital for prompts to be as specific as possible because, otherwise, the model will fill in the missing information itself, which is often not helpful.

The biggest caveat when using all generative AI is that hallucinations are inevitable, so every response must be taken with the requisite dose of salt. When generating code, triple-check the results because although GPT-4 is very good at crafting code, it's not perfect. Finally, when using ChatGPT to generate writing, it's a bad idea to use the result verbatim because although the text might look good from the point of view of just wanting to get a job finished, believe me when I say (even without seeing it) that the writing is tolerable at best and clichéd and boring at worst. If you hand in, submit, or publish AI-generated writing as-is, you're letting our new chatbot overlords win. Resist the temptation!

Chrissy LeMaire

The AI tool that I use is ChatGPT v4. Seriously, v3.5 just doesn't compare. Colleagues of mine who I've convinced to use ChatGPT try the free version, end up subscribing, and then reach out to tell me how the $20/month is so worth it.

I used to pay $10/month for a Midjourney subscription but now use the built-in DALL-E that comes with my OpenAI subscription. I like the output the same or better.

I also use krisp.ai (https://krisp.ai/) for my calls. Initially, I used it for sound isolation, but now that Mac does sound isolation, I use Krisp for the awesome meeting notes it generates after a call. The notes include summaries, to-dos, and highlights. So good.

A tip: if you're privacy conscious, you can prevent OpenAI from training on your queries. You can opt out at https://privacy.openai .com.

We're definitely going to figure this thing out . . . somehow

Leo Porter and Daniel Zingaro

In the computer science education research world right now, a lot of people are worried about students' overreliance on these tools. The concern is that students will use ChatGPT to get an answer but will then not reflect on or hone that answer or make that answer their own (in which case, a learning opportunity has been lost). We encourage readers to keep in mind each time they use a generative AI: What am I trying to achieve in terms of output and/or learning? Does this use align with those goals?

Nathan Crocker

The best advice that I can offer is, at least currently, always verify the result. If you are not familiar with the material, you can use an LLM as a springboard, but you should not treat it as the final authority. They are very good at generating the next series of convincing tokens, but that might not always be what you want. I recently attempted to copy Rust code for a basic API gateway out of ChatGPT (full disclosure, version 3.5), and it would not compile. YMMV (your mileage may vary).

Important definitions and a brief history

I'm afraid there's no way around it: if we want to get the *full* benefits of AI, we're going to have to swallow hard and absorb some serious concepts. Technology is complicated by design, and AI is a particularly complicated subset of technology. The good news is that we're not trying to qualify as physicists and engineers, so a very basic grasp of these ideas and their history will work just fine for our purposes. But prepare for some turbulence all the same.

Some critical AI definitions

To get you started, figure A.1 is helpful diagram illustrating the complex relationships between the many computational elements behind generative AI models.

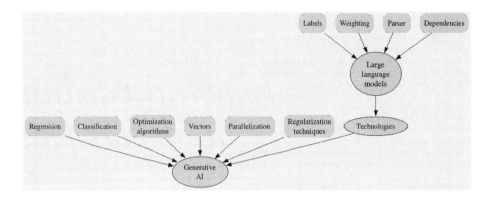

Figure A.1.   A left-to-right–oriented mindmap of AI relationships

Having said that, even if you choose to skip this section altogether, you'll still be able to successfully follow along with everything else in the book. However, you might have trouble identifying some of the nuances (and weaknesses) in the AI responses you get, and some instructions and processes may feel a bit arbitrary.

I should note that the definitions for many of these concepts will reference other concepts. I'll do my best to refer to only things that have been previously defined, but there are too many twisted (and recursive) relationships to make that happen every time. With that warning, here's some fundamental knowledge that'll make you more effective at working with generative AI.

Machine learning is a branch of artificial intelligence that focuses on developing algorithms and models capable of automatically learning and improving from data without explicit programming. It involves training a system on a large dataset to recognize patterns, make predictions, or perform tasks. By iteratively adjusting model parameters, machine learning enables computers to learn from experience and adapt to new inputs, enabling them to make informed decisions and perform complex tasks with minimal human intervention.

In the context of AI, a *model* refers to a mathematical representation or computational system that learns patterns, structures, or relationships from data. It's a trained algorithm or network that can take input and generate meaningful output based on its learned knowledge or trained parameters. In generative AI, a model refers specifically to a system that can generate new data samples that resemble the training data, whether it's generating images, text, music, or other forms of creative content. The model encapsulates the learned information and the ability to generate new instances based on that knowledge.

Labels are categorizations or annotations assigned to data points. They provide explicit information about the characteristics or attributes associated with the input. Labels act as guiding signals to help the model learn and generate output that aligns with the desired attributes or properties. One place where labels are commonly used is for sentiment analysis. Sentiment analysis involves training a model to classify text as either positive, negative, or neutral based on its emotional tone. To perform this task, we need to label our training data with appropriate sentiments (e.g., "This review is positive," "This tweet is negative").

Weighting refers to the numerical values assigned to the connections between neurons or features in a model. These weights determine the strength or importance of each connection and play a crucial role in the model's learning and decision-making process. During training, the weights are adjusted iteratively based on the observed errors or differences between predicted and actual outputs, enabling the model to learn from the data and improve its performance by assigning appropriate weights to different inputs and connections. Weighting is commonly used for named entity recognition (NER), which involves identifying and categorizing entities mentioned in text into predefined categories like person, organization, and location. A weighted NER model, for instance, can be used for a chatbot application to extract and respond to user queries about specific topics or entities.

A *parser* is a software component or algorithm that analyzes the structure of a given input, typically in the form of a sequence of symbols or text, and generates a structured representation based on a predefined grammar or set of rules. It is commonly used in natural language processing to parse sentences and extract syntactic or semantic information. Parsers break down the input into constituent parts, such as words or phrases, and establish relationships between them, enabling further analysis, understanding, or processing of the input data.

By understanding the *dependencies* between words, sentences, or visual elements, generative AI models can generate meaningful sequences or images that maintain contextual consistency. Modeling dependencies allows the generated output to exhibit logical flow, semantic coherence, and adherence to patterns observed in the training data. Accurately capturing dependencies is essential for generating high-quality and coherent outputs in generative AI applications.

Regression is a supervised machine learning technique used to predict or estimate a continuous output variable based on input features. It models the relationship between the input variables and the output variable by fitting a mathematical function to the training data. The goal is to find the best-fitting function that minimizes the difference between the predicted values and the actual values. Regression algorithms analyze the patterns and trends in the data to make predictions or infer relationships. Regression can be another tool for sentiment analysis. For customer service-related tasks, for instance, it's important to be able to automatically classify customer complaints or praise to allow organizations to accurately route issues to the appropriate support agents.

Classification is a fundamental task in machine learning where the goal is to assign input data points to predefined categories or classes. It involves training a model on labeled data, where each data point is associated with a known class. The model learns patterns and relationships in the training data to make predictions on new, unseen data. The output of a classification model is a discrete class label that represents the predicted category to which the input belongs.

Optimization algorithms are mathematical procedures used to find the optimal solution for a given problem. In the context of machine learning and neural networks, these algorithms are employed to minimize an objective function, typically represented by a loss or cost function. The goal is to adjust the model's parameters iteratively to reach the optimal set of values that minimize the objective function. In the world of optimizing models, there are some popular techniques like stochastic gradient descent and its variations. These methods help the model get better by adjusting its internal settings according to how much it's improving or getting worse. By doing this, the model gets closer to finding the best possible solution and performs much better at its tasks.

Vectors are mathematical entities used to represent both magnitude and direction in a multidimensional space. In the context of machine learning and data analysis, vectors are often used to represent features or data points. Each dimension of a vector corresponds to a specific attribute or variable, allowing for efficient storage and manipulation of data. Vectors can be operated upon using mathematical operations like addition, subtraction, and dot product, enabling calculations of similarity, distances, and transformations. Vectors play a fundamental role in various algorithms and models, such as clustering, classification, and dimensionality reduction.

Vector embeddings help LLMs generalize knowledge across similar words and phrases, even if they weren't encountered during training. This allows the model to handle out-of-vocabulary words effectively. Pretrained embeddings can be used as starting points for various NLP tasks, enabling transfer learning and improving performance on downstream tasks with limited data. One practical application of all this would be medical imaging, where vector embeddings can be used to analyze and compare images of organs or tissues. A deep learning model can be trained to map brain scans onto a vector space, where similar scans are clustered together. This enables doctors to quickly identify patterns and abnormalities in patient scans, leading to earlier diagnosis and treatment of diseases such as cancer or neurological disorders.

Word embeddings are a way of representing words as vectors in a high-dimensional space, such that similar words are close together in that space. Word embeddings are typically represented as tensors, where each dimension represents a different aspect of the word's meaning. For example, a word embedding tensor might have dimensions for the word's synonyms, antonyms, and part of speech.

Parallelization refers to the technique of dividing a computational task into smaller subtasks that can be executed simultaneously on multiple computing resources. It leverages the power of parallel processing to speed up the overall computation and improve efficiency. In parallel computing, tasks are allocated to different processors, threads, or computing units, allowing them to work concurrently. This approach enables tasks to be completed faster by distributing the workload across multiple resources. Parallelization is widely used in various fields, including machine learning, scientific simulations, and data processing, to achieve significant performance gains and handle large-scale computations efficiently.

Regularization techniques are methods used to improve the generalization performance of models. These techniques add a penalty term to the loss function during training, discouraging the model from relying too heavily on complex or noisy patterns in the data. Regularization techniques help control model complexity, reduce overfitting, and improve the model's ability to generalize to unseen data.

A common practical application of regularization techniques is in text classification, specifically when dealing with imbalanced datasets. Let's say we have a dataset of movie reviews, where the majority class is positive reviews (e.g., "good movie") and the minority class is negative reviews (e.g., "bad movie"). Without regularization, the model might become biased toward the positive reviews and fail to accurately classify the negative reviews. To address this imbalance, we can add a regularization term to the loss function that penalizes the model for misclassifying negative reviews.

Convergence refers to the process of training multiple models on the same dataset until they produce similar outputs. This is done to reduce the risk of overfitting and improve the generalization of the models. Convergence is typically evaluated using metrics such as validation loss or accuracy, and the training process is stopped once the models converge to a stable solution.

All of this brings us to *natural language processing* (NLP). NLP focuses on the interaction between computers and human language. It involves the development of algorithms and models to enable computers to understand, interpret, and generate human language in a meaningful way. NLP encompasses tasks such as text classification, sentiment analysis, machine translation, information extraction, and question answering. It uses techniques from various disciplines, including computational linguistics, machine learning, and deep learning, to process and analyze textual data.

And, finally, we arrive at a *large language model* (LLM). LLM is a tool in natural language processing (NLP) that uses deep learning techniques to understand and generate human-like text. It analyzes patterns, contexts, and semantics within a given text corpus to learn the underlying structures of language. With its ability to comprehend and generate coherent and contextually relevant responses, an LLM can be used for various tasks, such as chatbots, language translation, text completion, and summarization. By capturing the intricacies of language, an LLM allows machines to communicate directly with humans. In other words, it enables generative AI.

I'll finish up this appendix with a bit of technology history.

A very (very) brief history of AI

Why *so very* brief? Because I know you're impatient and because I'm going to leave out any dates, concepts, events, and technical breakthroughs that won't help us reach our only goal here: AI productivity. Figure A.2 gives you a visual overview of what we're going to see.

1950	The Turing Test
1954	The Georgetown-IBM experiment
1957	A perceptron
1992	The Q-learning algorithm
1998	Support vector machines (SVMs)
2012	Deep convolutional neural network (AlexNet)
2014	Generative adversarial networks (GANs)
2017	The transformer model
2017	The Mask R-CNN model

Figure A.2.   A timeline tracking the history of artificial intelligence

At any rate, I guess "the beginning" would be 1950, when mathematician and computer pioneer Alan Turing proposed the Turing test as a measure of machine intelligence. Could a computer engage in conversation with humans without them being able to tell that they weren't conversing with a real person? Or, in other words, could a computer at least appear to think and communicate like a human?

The year 1954 saw the first machine-based language translation tool as part of a Georgetown-IBM experiment. Using a crude methodology, dozens of Russian sentences were translated into English.

Next up? A *perceptron*, first introduced in 1957, is a software algorithm used as a fundamental building block of neural networks and an early form of artificial neuron. It's a mathematical model inspired by the way biological neurons function in the human brain. Each artificial neuron receives input signals, applies weights to them, and passes the sum through an activation function to produce an output. By adjusting the weights through a process called training, neural networks can learn complex patterns and relationships in data.

A perceptron takes multiple input signals, applies weights to those inputs, sums them up, and applies an activation function to produce an output. Perceptrons are often organized into layers, forming multilayer perceptrons (MLPs) or feedforward neural networks. By stacking multiple perceptrons together and connecting them in complex patterns, neural networks can learn and model more intricate relationships and solve a wide range of problems, including pattern recognition, classification, and regression tasks.

Here is a simplified illustration of a perceptron:

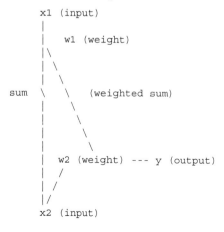

```
x1 (input)
|
|    w1 (weight)
|\
| \
|  \
sum \   \    (weighted sum)
|    \
|     \
|      \
|       \
|   w2 (weight) --- y (output)
|   /
| /
|/
x2 (input)
```

In this example, a perceptron takes two inputs ($x1$ and $x2$) with corresponding weights ($w1$ and $w2$). The inputs are multiplied by their respective weights and then summed together. The weighted sum is then passed through an activation function (not shown) to produce the output (y). The perceptron calculates the output based on the weighted sum of the inputs and the activation function.

Yeah. I don't completely understand that either. But what's important for us is that software was being used to process enormous volumes of data in ways that made intelligence-like insights possible.

An early natural language parser (creatively called SHRDLU) was developed in 1971 by Terry Winograd. This was important because it used a rules-based system to allow a computer to draw conclusions about relationships and attributes without necessarily having any real understanding of its actual environment.

In 1992, Chris Watkins introduced the Q-learning algorithm, paving the way for reinforcement learning techniques. Reinforcement learning is where a software agent learns through trial and error by interacting with an environment, receiving rewards or penalties for its actions. The goal is to maximize cumulative reward by discovering optimal strategies or policies.

The late 1990s saw the beginnings of support vector machines (SVMs). SVMs are a supervised machine learning algorithm used for classification and regression tasks. Classification is particularly important to us because separating objects and events into classes allows computers to better predict relationships and outcomes. Remember, computers don't *know* anything. But they can draw conclusions based on measurable relationships.

Supervised machine learning, by the way, is where a model learns from labeled training data, consisting of input features and corresponding output labels. It aims to map input-output relationships, enabling the model to make predictions or classify new, unseen data based on the patterns learned from the labeled examples.

In 2012, the deep convolutional neural network AlexNet, achieved a breakthrough in image classification accuracy that kickstarted the deep learning revolution. Curious about deep learning? Well, it's a subset of machine learning that uses artificial neural networks with multiple layers to learn hierarchical representations of data. It excels at extracting intricate patterns, recognizing complex features, and achieving high performance in tasks like image recognition, natural language processing, and speech synthesis. All important stuff.

In 2014, generative adversarial networks (GANs) were introduced by Ian Goodfellow and colleagues, revolutionizing generative modeling. GANs are a class of machine learning models that consist of two neural networks—namely, the generator and the discriminator, engaged in a competitive learning process. The *adversarial* part of the name comes from the fact that the generator and discriminator are trained simultaneously in an adversarial manner. The generator aims to produce increasingly realistic data to fool the discriminator, while the discriminator improves its ability to distinguish real from fake data. The main value of generative modeling is the ability to generate new, realistic data that resembles a training set. This has several applications, including data augmentation, creative content generation, data synthesis, and novelty detection (meaning, the identification of statistical outliers and anomalies).

By 2017, attention-based models, such as the transformer model, revolutionized machine translation and natural language processing tasks, had been developed. A transformer architecture is a special kind of advanced learning model that uses self-attention mechanisms to understand relationships between different parts of information presented in a sequence. This has had a significant effect on tasks involving natural language, like understanding and translating languages. It works more efficiently by handling multiple pieces of information at once (parallelization) and learning the context of words or phrases (contextual representations), which has made language-related tasks much better and faster.

Just what is deep learning? It's a methodology that uses artificial neural networks with multiple layers to learn hierarchical representations of data. It excels at capturing complex patterns, recognizing intricate features, and tasks such as image recognition, natural language processing, and speech synthesis.

The transformer model has been a game changer. Don't believe me? When I asked ChatGPT itself to identify the innovation that drove its success the most, it replied, "The application of the transformer architecture."

Self-attention mechanisms allow models to focus on different parts of input sequences when processing them. By comparing each input element to all other elements, self-attention determines the importance or relevance of different positions within the sequence. This enables the model to weigh and aggregate information effectively, capturing dependencies and learning contextual representations. Self-attention has been instrumental in improving natural language processing tasks.

Also in 2017, the Mask R-CNN model, combining object detection and instance segmentation, represented a leap forward in computer vision. Mask R-CNN is a deep-learning model for object detection and instance segmentation tasks. Building on the Faster R-CNN architecture, it adds a mask prediction branch to identify pixel-level object masks.

While it's far too recent to be characterized as "history," we can't move on without at least mentioning the role played by OpenAI in all this. OpenAI is an artificial intelligence research organization and technology company. It was founded in December 2015 with the goal of developing and promoting widespread use of AI through innovations in AI technologies.

OpenAI is known for its development of language models, such as Generative Pre-trained Transformer (GPT). Through their impressive capabilities in natural language processing and generation, OpenAI models have captured significant public attention, leading to mass adoption of AI for the first time in history.

Initially, OpenAI focused on publishing its research and making it accessible to the wider community. However, due to concerns about potential misuse of AI, OpenAI introduced a revised approach, emphasizing a balance between sharing research and safeguarding against risks through initiatives that include advocating for government regulation. Some would say that this shift reflects OpenAI's commitment to ensuring the responsible and ethical use of AI technology. (Others of a more cynical bent would suggest that making it harder for new startups to enter the market offers the greatest benefits to early industry leaders, like OpenAI.)

Generative AI resources

By now, I'm sure you've noticed how fast things change in the AI world. Announcements from the big players of new features for their flagship products come nearly daily. But there are also frequent news about new third-party applications making innovative use of existing platforms and new and creative ways of working with the tools we already have.

I used to try to keep on top of it all. But that didn't work out well.

Nevertheless, it's important to stay at least broadly familiar with as much of what's out there as possible. With that in mind, this appendix contains links to a few examples of tools covering all the main categories of AI and AI-adjacent tools. As this won't stay fresh for long, I also created a GitHub repo (https://mng.bz/eoVJ), where I plan to regularly update the contents of this appendix with new resources.

To be honest, my definition of *regularly* might not always match your expectations, so feel free to open a Git issue or drop me a note (office@bootstrap-it.com) with any categories or up-and-coming tool that I might have missed (or willfully ignored). Just bear in mind that this list is not meant to include *every single* AI tool out there. Rather, it's a place where we can all check back from time to time to make sure we're not missing any important new functionality.

General LLM interaction tools

- OpenAI GPT Playground (https://platform.openai.com/ playground)
- LLaMa Chat (https://labs.perplexity.ai/)
- Stack Overflow AI (https://mng.bz/Y7V7)
- Anthropic (Claude) (https://mng.bz/GZNN)
- LangChain (https://www.langchain.com/)
- ChatGPT with enterprise-grade security and privacy (https:// openai.com/enterprise)
- GPT for Sheets plugin—Get GPT to generate content within Google Sheets and Docs (https://mng.bz/z8nZ)
- Groq (https://groq.com/)
- NVIDIA ChatRTX—Nvidia's locally-hosted desktop Gen AI tool (Windows 11 only right now) (https://www.nvidia.com/ en-us/ai-on-rtx/chatrtx/)

AI application development platforms

- Hugging Face (https://huggingface.co/)
- Generative AI on AWS (https://aws.amazon.com/ generative-ai/)
- Azure OpenAI Service (https://mng.bz/0GMz)
- Google Cloud AI Platform (https://mng.bz/KZDn)
- Google Colaboratory—A host for Jupyter Notebook workflows (https://colab.google/)
- Google's Project IDX—A browser-based, AI-powered development environment for building full-stack and multiplatform applications (https://mng.bz/9do8)
- GPT-3.5 Turbo fine-tuning (https://mng.bz/jX09)

Third-party tools

- ChatPDF (https://www.chatpdf.com/)
- Botpress—A no-code tool for building GPT-based customer support chatbots (https://botpress.com/)

Writing tools

- Copy.ai (https://www.copy.ai/)
- Ryttr (https://rytr.me/)
- GrammarlyGo (https://www.grammarly.com/a/grammarlygo)
- Writesonic (https://writesonic.com/)

Image generation

- Midjourney (https://www.midjourney.com/)
- StyleGAN—Powerful, but requires a high-end NVIDIA GPU, etc. (https://github.com/NVlabs/stylegan)
- Canva AI—Incorporates text prompts into your Canva workflow (https://www.canva.com/ai-image-generator/)
- AI Comic Factory—Generates comic book panels from text prompts (https://mng.bz/WEVX)
- Leonardo AI—Limited access at this time (https://leonardo.ai/)
- Craiyon—A free AI image generator (https://www.craiyon.com/)

Data analytics

- OpenAI Codex (https://openai.com/blog/openai-codex/)
- Datagran—AI chat data scientist (https://www.datagran.io/)

Investment and financial

- Portfolio Pilot (https://portfoliopilot.com/portfolio)
- composer (https://www.composer.trade/)

Speech-to-text

- Whisper (OpenAI) (https://github.com/openai/whisper)
- otter.ai—Live transcriptions or notes from meetings, lectures, or conversations (https://otter.ai/)

Text-to-speech

- Amazon Polly (https://aws.amazon.com/polly/)
- CereProc (https://www.cereproc.com/)
- WellSaid Labs (https://wellsaidlabs.com/)
- Microsoft Azure (https://mng.bz/8w6g)
- IBM Watson (https://mng.bz/EZOr)

Text-to-music

- Mubert (https://mubert.com/)
- AIVA (https://www.aiva.ai/)
- boomy (https://boomy.com/)
- Soundful (https://soundful.com/)

Text-to-video

- Gen-2 Runway Research (https://research.runwayml.com/gen2)

Text-to-video presentations (including animated and lifelike avatars)

- Synthesia.io—Outstanding quality but very expensive (https://www.synthesia.io/)
- elai (https://elai.io/)
- Fliki—No avatar, but good focus on blog-to-video workflow (https://fliki.ai/)

Slide deck generation

- Gamma— Generates docs, decks, and webpages from text (https://gamma.app/)
- Also, check out the many third-party integrations with Google Slides. From the Google Play site, search for "AI slide maker."

Text, audio, and video language translation

- Seamless Communication Translation— A free demo of Meta's speech translation tool that supports nearly 100 input and 35 output languages (https://seamless.metademolab.com/)
- SeamlessM4T—Developer's version of Meta's multimodal translation tool (https://mng.bz/NRBX)
- HayGen—Translates the audio within videos to a different language; includes updated lip-syncing (https://labs.heygen.com/video-translate)

Domain specific

- Harvey—A law-aware AI service (https://www.harvey.ai/)
- Speech therapy—Still experimental! (https://www.betterspeech.com/jessica)

Installing Python

In case you need to do this manually, here are guides for installing Python and `pip` on Windows, macOS, and Linux machines.

Installing Python on Windows

To download the Python package, go to the official Python website (https://www.python.org/downloads/windows/). Make sure you're downloading the latest version (at the time of writing, it's Python 3.x). Choose the appropriate version based on your system architecture (32-bit or 64-bit). Most modern computers are 64-bit, but you can confirm by right-clicking This PC (or My Computer) and selecting Properties.

Once the installer is downloaded, run it. Check the box that says Add Python x.x to PATH. This will make it easier to run Python and `pip` from the command prompt. Then click Install Now.

You can verify your installation by opening the command prompt by pressing Win + R, typing `cmd`, and then pressing Enter. To check whether Python was installed successfully, type `python --version` and press Enter. You should see the version number displayed.

`pip` is usually included with recent versions of Python. To check whether `pip` is already installed, type `pip --version` in the command prompt and press Enter. If you see version information, you have `pip` installed; otherwise, you need to install it manually.

To get that done, download the `get-pip.py` script from the official Python Packaging Authority site (https://bootstrap.pypa.io/get-pip.py) and save the script to a location on your computer. Open the command prompt and navigate to the directory where you saved `get-pip.py` using the `cd` command. For example,

```
cd C:\Users\YourUsername\Downloads
```

Then run this command:

```
python get-pip.py
```

To verify your pip Installation, run `pip --version` in the command prompt.

With Python and `pip` installed, you can install packages using the command `pip install package-name`.

Installing Python on macOS

macOS usually comes with a pre-installed version of Python. To check whether Python is already installed, open the terminal (you can find it in the Applications > Utilities folder) and type

```
python3 --version
```

If you see a version number, you have Python installed. If not, complete the following steps to install it.

Homebrew is a popular package manager for macOS that makes installing software easier. If you don't have Homebrew installed, you can install it using the following command in the terminal:

```
/bin/bash -c "$(curl -fsSL \
  https://raw.githubusercontent.com/Homebrew/install/master/install.sh)"
Install Python 3:
```

If you're using Homebrew, you can install Python 3 by running the following command in the terminal:

```
brew install python
```

If you're not using Homebrew, you can download the official Python installer from the Python website (https://www.python.org/downloads/mac-osx/).

Here's what you'll need to do:

1 Download the latest version of Python 3.x.
2 Run the installer package you downloaded and follow the installation instructions.
3 Verify Installation.

After installing, you should be able to access Python by typing `python3` in the terminal, and verifying the installed version with `python3 --version`.

Python 3 usually comes with `pip` pre-installed. To verify whether `pip` is installed, run

`pip3 --version`

If you see version information, you're all set. If not, you can install `pip` manually:

1 Download the `get-pip.py` script (https://bootstrap.pypa.io/get-pip.py).
2 Open the terminal and navigate to the directory where you saved `get-pip.py` using the `cd` command. For example, `cd ~/Downloads`
3 Run the following command: `sudo python3 get-pip.py`.

After `pip` is installed, you can check its version by running `pip3 --version` in the terminal.

With Python and `pip` installed, you can start using Python and installing packages from PyPI. To install packages, use the command `pip3 install package-name`.

Remember that you might need to use `python3` and `pip3` in the terminal (rather than `python` and `pip`) to ensure you're using Python 3 and its associated pip.

Installing the pip Python package manager on Linux

Please note that some Linux distributions come with Python pre-installed, so it's a good idea to check first before installing a new version. To do that, open a terminal and type

```
python3 --version
```

If you see a version number, you have Python installed. If not, complete the following steps to install it.

It's a good practice to update your package manager before installing software. For systems using `apt` (Debian/Ubuntu), use

```
sudo apt update
```

For systems using `dnf` (Fedora), use

```
sudo dnf update
```

To install Python 3, use the package manager. That'll mean either `sudo apt install python3` or `sudo dnf install python3`, depending on your system. The package name might differ slightly depending on your distribution.

After installing, you should be able to access Python 3 by typing `python3` in the terminal using

```
python3 --version.
```

Python 3 usually comes with `pip` pre-installed. To verify whether `pip` is installed, run

```
pip3 --version
```

If you see version information, you're all set. If not, you can install `pip` manually using either `sudo apt install python3-pip` or `sudo dnf install python3-pip` Again, the `3` part of those commands may, on some systems, be the default setting, so you might need to leave the `3` out.

After `pip` is installed, you can check its version by running `pip3 --version` in the terminal. With Python and `pip` installed, you can start using Python and installing packages from PyPI. To install packages, use the `command pip3 install package-name`.

index

211